BACKYARD BIRDS OF TEXAS

By Michael Harrell, M.S.

© Michael T Harrell, M.S., all rights reserved.

No part of this book may be reproduced, stored, or transmitted by any means without the written permission of the author.

Published December 2023

Dedication

To my wife (Angela) for her love, dedication, and support.

And

To my dear niece Abby Harrell
We will always love you.

CONTENTS

Page	Topic
10	About the Author
13	About this Book
14	How to Identify Birds
20	Acadian Flycatcher
21	American Crow
22	American Goldfinch
23	American Kestrel
24	American Pipit
25	American Redstart
26	American Robin
27	American Tree Sparrow
28	Ash-throated Flycatcher
29	Baltimore Oriole
30	Bank Swallow
31	Barn Owl
32	Barn Swallow
33	Barred Owl
34	Bell's Vireo
35	Bewick's Wren
36	Black-and-white Warbler
37	Black-capped Vireo
38	Black-chinned Hummingbird
39	Black-crested Titmouse
40	Black-headed Grosbeak
41	Black-tailed Gnatcatcher
42	Black-throated Sparrow
43	Blue-gray Gnatcatcher
44	Blue Grosbeak
45	Blue-headed Vireo
46	Blue Jay
47	Brewer's Blackbird
48	Brewer's Sparrow
49	Broad-winged Hawk

50	Bronzed Cowbird
51	Brown Creeper
52	Brown-crested Flycatcher
53	Brown-headed Cowbird
54	Brown-headed Nuthatch
55	Brown Thrasher
56	Bullock's Oriole
57	Bushtit
58	Cactus Wren
59	Canyon Towhee
60	Canyon Wren
61	Carolina Chickadee
62	Carolina Wren
63	Cassin's Sparrow
64	Cedar Waxwing
65	Chestnut-collared Longspur
66	Chihuahuan Raven
67	Chimney Swift
68	Chipping Sparrow
69	Clay-colored Sparrow
70	Cliff Swallow
71	Common Ground Dove
72	Common Grackle
73	Common Raven
74	Common Yellowthroat
75	Cooper's Hawk
76	Couch's Kingbird
77	Crested Caracara
78	Curve-billed Thrasher
79	Dark-eyed Junco
80	Dickcissel
81	Downy Woodpecker
82	Eastern Bluebird
83	Eastern Kingbird
84	Eastern Meadowlark

85	Eastern Phoebe
86	Eastern Screech-Owl
87	Eastern Towhee
88	Eastern Wood-Pewee
89	Elf Owl
90	Eurasian Collared-Dove
91	European Starling
92	Evening Grosbeak
93	Ferruginous Hawk
94	Field Sparrow
95	Fox Sparrow
96	Golden-cheeked Warbler
97	Golden-crowned Kinglet
98	Golden-fronted Woodpecker
99	Grasshopper Sparrow
100	Gray Catbird
101	Gray Hawk
102	Great-crested Flycatcher
103	Greater Roadrunner
104	Great Horned Owl
105	Great-tailed Grackle
106	Green Jay
107	Green Kingfisher
108	Green-tailed Towhee
109	Hairy Woodpecker
110	Harris's Hawk
111	Harris's Sparrow
112	Hepatic Tanager
113	Hermit Thrush
114	Hooded Oriole
115	Horned Lark
116	House Finch
117	House Sparrow
118	House Wren
119	Inca Dove

120	Indigo Bunting
121	Ladder-backed Woodpecker
122	Lark Bunting
123	Lark Sparrow
124	Lazuli Bunting
125	Least Flycatcher
126	LeConte's Sparrow
127	Lesser Goldfinch
128	Lincoln's Sparrow
129	Loggerhead Shrike
130	Long-billed Thrasher
131	Long-eared Owl
132	Louisiana Waterthrush
133	MacGillivray's Warbler
134	Marsh Wren
135	Mississippi Kite
136	Mountain Bluebird
137	Mourning Dove
138	Nashville Warbler
139	Northern Cardinal
140	Northern Flicker
141	Northern Mockingbird
142	Northern Parula
143	Northern Rough-winged Swallow
144	Northern Waterthrush
145	Olive-sided Flycatcher
146	Olive Sparrow
147	Orange-crowned Warbler
148	Orchard Oriole
149	Ovenbird
150	Painted Bunting
151	Pileated Woodpecker
152	Pine Siskin
153	Pine Warbler
154	Prairie Falcon

155	Prothonotary Warbler
156	Purple Martin
157	Pyrrhuloxia
158	Red-bellied Woodpecker
159	Red-breasted Nuthatch
160	Red Crossbill
161	Red-eyed Vireo
162	Red-headed Woodpecker
163	Red-shouldered Hawk
164	Red-tailed Hawk
165	Red-winged Blackbird
166	Rock Wren
167	Rose-breasted Grosbeak
168	Rough-legged Hawk
169	Ruby-crowned Kinglet
170	Ruby-throated Hummingbird
171	Rufous-crowned Sparrow
172	Rufous Hummingbird
173	Rusty Blackbird
174	Sage Thrasher
175	Savannah Sparrow
176	Say's Phoebe
177	Scarlet Tanager
178	Scissor-tailed Flycatcher
179	Scott's Oriole
180	Sharp-shinned Hawk
181	Short-eared Owl
182	Song Sparrow
183	Spotted Towhee
184	Summer Tanager
185	Swallow-tailed Kite
186	Swamp Sparrow
187	Townsend's Warbler
188	Tree Swallow
189	Tufted Titmouse

190	Varied Bunting
191	Verdin
192	Vermilion Flycatcher
193	Vesper Sparrow
194	Violet-green Swallow
195	Warbling Vireo
196	Western Kingbird
197	Western Meadowlark
198	Western Screech-Owl
199	Western Tanager
200	Western Wood-Pewee
201	White-breasted Nuthatch
202	White-crowned Sparrow
203	White-eyed Vireo
204	White-tailed Kite
205	White-throated Sparrow
206	White-tipped Dove
207	White-winged Dove
208	Willow Flycatcher
209	Wilson's Warbler
210	Winter Wren
211	Woodhouse's Scrub-Jay
212	Yellow-bellied Sapsucker
213	Yellow-billed Cuckoo
214	Yellow-breasted Chat
215	Yellow-headed Blackbird
216	Yellow-rumped Warbler
217	Yellow-throated Vireo
218	Yellow-throated Warbler
219	Yellow Warbler
220	Zone-tailed Hawk
221	References

ABOUT THE AUTHOR

A little about me. My name is Michael Harrell, and I have either been in college or teaching college since 1986. I have a Master of Science in Biology, and I have worked with everything from alligator snapping turtles to human anatomy and physiology. I have been preparing students seeking careers in health care and biology for over 20 years. In this time, I have been teaching the following:
- Human Anatomy and Physiology lecture parts one and two.
- Human Anatomy and Physiology lab parts one and two.
- Pathophysiology which is how disease affects the body.
- Nutrition   - Genetics   - Biology   - Zoology and more

I have published college level study guides on Human Anatomy & Physiology, Histology (the study of tissues), children's books on Human Anatomy and Physiology, children's education, Louisiana animals, and more. My work is available on Amazon.com. Search **"Harrell anatomy"** or the book title, and my books will be visible.

Books I have written.

Study Guide to Human Anatomy and Physiology 1
Study Guide to Human Anatomy and Physiology 2
Histology Lab Atlas
The Heart and Heart Problems   My First Anatomy Book
The ABCs of Human Anatomy and Physiology
Learning About Animals the ABC Way
My Crazy Bug Book   The Greatest Dinosaur Collection of All Time
Wildflowers of Louisiana   Animals of the Louisiana Bayou
Ducks of Louisiana   Ducks of Texas   Ducks of Florida
Ducks of California   Ducks of New York   Ducks of Canada
Backyard Birds of Louisiana, 2nd Edition
Raptors of Louisiana   Game Birds of Louisiana
Butterflies of Louisiana   Wildflowers of Louisiana
Snakes of Louisiana   Ducks of North America

I was born and raised in the woods and on the waters of Louisiana. Like many people here, much of our lives revolve around hunting and fishing. I have had the unique perspective of growing up with these animals and learning more about them as I studied to become a biologist.

If you travel around the U.S., you quickly discover how Louisiana is unique. From what I have seen, we have more wildlife and a greater diversity of it than any other location in North America. If we consider why that is, the answer can be found in two words: water and heat. Nowhere else on this continent does any area have the quantity of water and so many warm days as Louisiana does. Water and warmth are the two biggest factors when it comes to life, so with an abundance of those two things, we have an abundance of life.

I couldn't count how many times we had students come to school in Louisiana from other parts of the country and world and make the comment, "I've never seen so many animals." When you grow up here, we take our incredible amount of wildlife for granted. Whether it's insects, fish, amphibians, reptiles, or mammals, Louisiana truly is a sportsman's paradise.

A few of my books available on Amazon.com

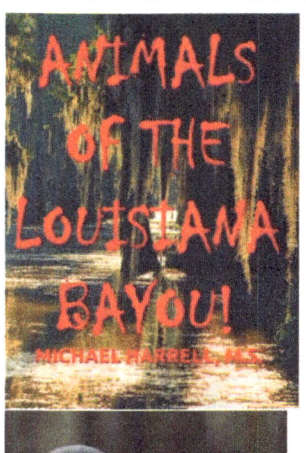

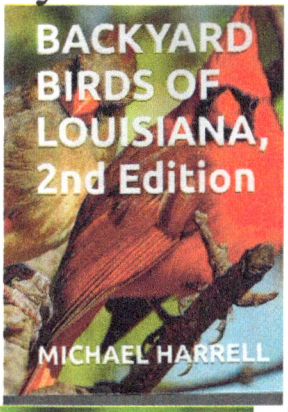

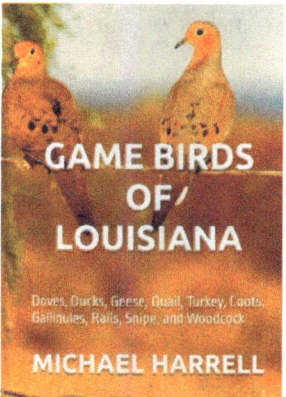

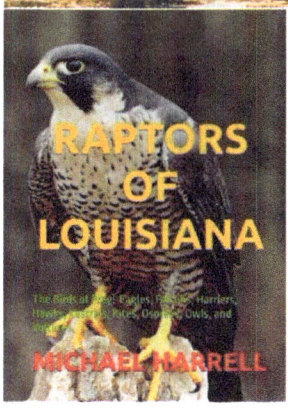

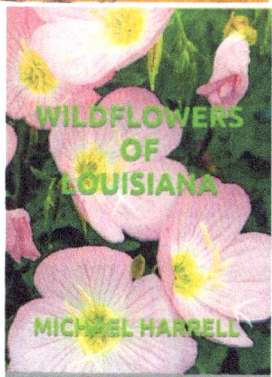

LEARNING ABOUT ANIMALS THE ABC WAY!
MICHAEL HARRELL, M.S.

MY FIRST ANATOMY BOOK!
ACTIVITIES FOR KIDS
Michael Harrell M.S.
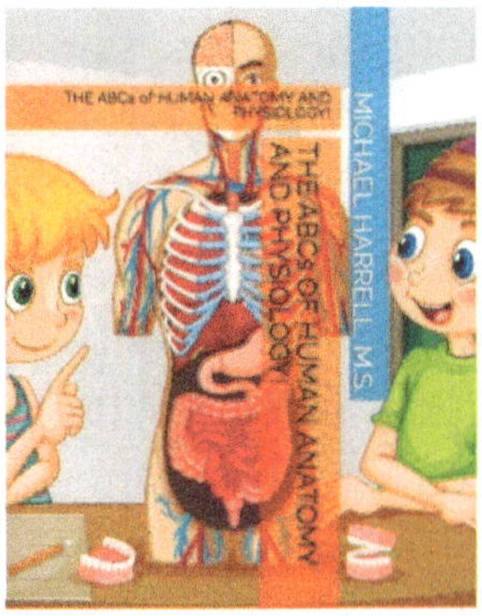
THE ABCs of HUMAN ANATOMY AND PHYSIOLOGY!
THE ABCs OF HUMAN ANATOMY AND PHYSIOLOGY
MICHAEL HARRELL M.S.
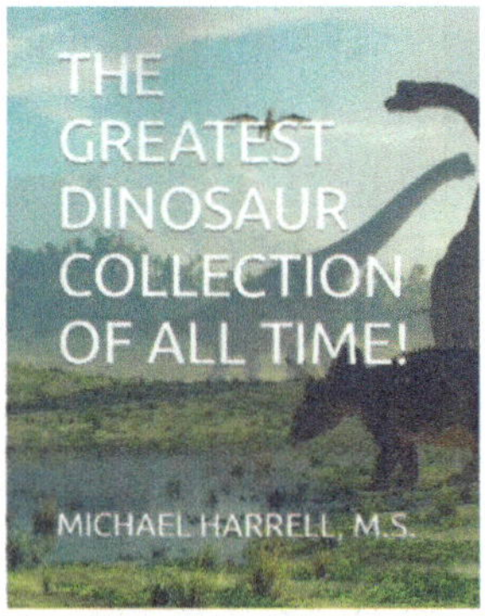
THE GREATEST DINOSAUR COLLECTION OF ALL TIME!
MICHAEL HARRELL, M.S.
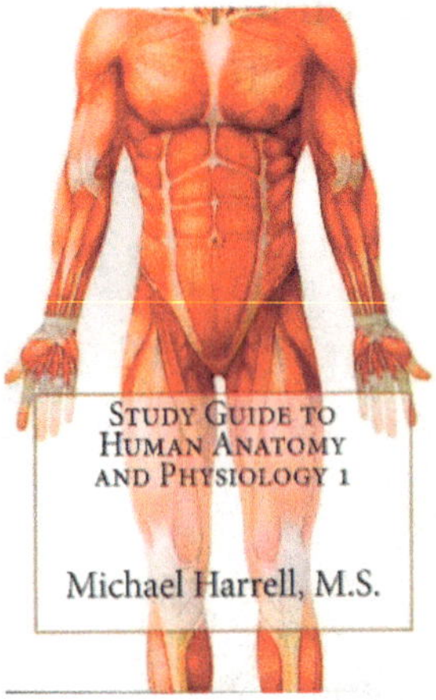
Study Guide to Human Anatomy and Physiology 1
Michael Harrell, M.S.

Study Guide to Human Anatomy and Physiology 2
Michael Harrell, M.S.
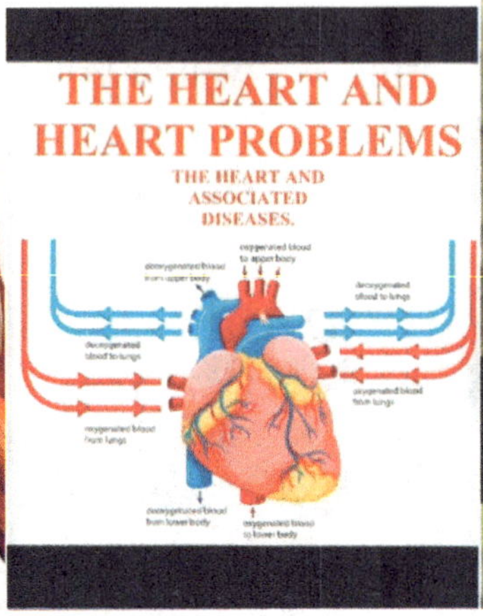
THE HEART AND HEART PROBLEMS
THE HEART AND ASSOCIATED DISEASES.

Histology Lab Atlas
2nd Edition
Michael Harrell, M.S.

DUCKS OF CALIFORNIA
MICHAEL HARRELL

DUCKS OF FLORIDA
MICHAEL HARRELL

DUCKS OF TEXAS
MICHAEL HARRELL, M.S.

MICHAEL HARRELL
DUCKS OF NEW YORK
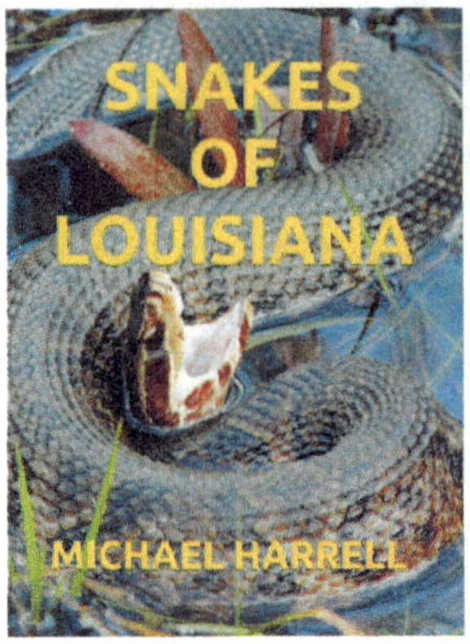
SNAKES OF LOUISIANA
MICHAEL HARRELL

DUCKS OF NORTH AMERICA
MICHAEL HARRELL

About this Book

Texas contains around 670 species of birds. Some of them are with us year round, and some visit us at certain times of the year. We won't try to cover them all, but we will look at some of the more familiar and interesting species. This book will cover most backyard birds seen in your yards, trees, bushes, at your feeders, and more.

Some of these birds you will recognize immediately, and you may see them in your yard daily. Some will be seasonal visitors and may be birds you associate with particular times of the year. Some birds are signs of spring, and some are signs of winter.

In this book, you will find great color pictures, detailed descriptions, information on sounds, diet, and more. I hope you will use this to identify the birds you see and enjoy those birds even more.

American Redstart shown below.

How to Identify Birds

Learning how to identify birds can be a bit difficult at first. To accurately identify a bird, we first need to know what to look for. This will often require relearning what we currently do when looking for identifying characteristics. We often go first to colors, but we will see that other characteristics are more beneficial to look at first. Below, we will take key items one at a time and discuss them.

Groups of birds.
Birds can be separated into many groups, and the number of groups will vary depending on your source. Some sources will identify as many as 30 bird groups, and others may use as few as twelve.

When looking at a bird, consider first whether it has the shape of a sparrow, owl, hawk, duck, etc. With backyard birds, consider whether they have the shape of a blackbird, chickadee, crow, jay, dove, finch, flycatcher, hawk, hummingbird, nuthatch, owl, sparrow, swallow, thrush, warbler, woodpecker, wren, and more. Consider the bird group first and then work from there. For example, if you get the bird down to the owl group, that will greatly limit your choices of what the bird could be.

Body shape of bird.
Knowing the overall body shape of a bird will help you place it in the proper group and greatly reduce the choices you have for identification. This will allow you to put the bird in the group we mentioned above, and from there you will have far fewer choices.

Let's compare the body shape of a sparrow to that of a hawk or an owl to that of a goose. Many of us already know the overall shape of many birds. Learn these shapes, and you can quickly put a bird into a group and then learn the groups one at a time. This is a good way to eliminate your choices when bird watching.

Size.
Compare the bird you see to a bird you are familiar with. You probably already have a general idea about the size of a hummingbird, a sparrow, a robin, an owl, a goose, and an eagle. Use that size to narrow down your bird options when identifying one you see.

Wing shape.
Bird wings are separated into groups:
1. Elliptical Wings – Elliptical wings are found on birds that need to make rapid changes in direction or fly short distances at high speed. Birds found largely in forests and those that don't migrate tend to have this wing shape. Many of the backyard perching birds fit into this group. Doves, woodpeckers, sparrows, and similar birds will have this wing shape.

2. High-Speed Wings – High speed wings will be long, slender, and pointed. They are of course needed on birds that would make a high speed attack or escape. These wings aren't as long as those found on the high soaring birds. Falcons and ducks are good examples of birds with this wing shape.

3. Active Soaring Wings – Active soaring wings are long and narrow. These wings are good for flying on air currents and traveling long distances. For this wing shape, think about ocean birds that are always gliding on the ocean breeze

and occasionally flapping. Gulls and albatrosses are good examples of birds with this wing shape.

4. Passive Soaring Wings – Passive soaring wings have primary feathers that greatly fan out with slots in between them. These wings are good for catching thermals (rising columns of air). Think about very large birds like eagles and buzzards for this wing type.

5. Hovering Wings – This wing type is good for wings that need to move very fast and allow the bird to fly in one spot. The Ruby-throated Hummingbird has this wing shape.

Bird Feathers.

Birds have many types of feathers. The structure, location, and function are different for each. The wing feathers are often the first ones we notice. Take note of their length, shape, color, and any other characteristics. Some, like tail feathers, can be short, long, curled, and of course have many colors.

Wing feathers.

Wingtips are found furthest from the bird's body and often have distinct colored borders. The flexible wingtips don't break as easily as others. For birds moving through trees, this probably allows the flexibility needed to keep them from breaking easily as they hit tree limbs.

The **trailing edge** is the rear part of the wing. The edge that air last passes over as a wing goes through the air.

The **leading edge** is the front edge of the wing. The edge that first strikes the air when the bird is flying.

Primary wing feathers are the outer wing feathers. Primary wing feathers are elongated, have finger-like tips, pointed tips, and very long quills. Most birds have nine to ten primary feathers. Primaries are attached to bones in the bird's hand. These feathers are rigid and are used for thrusting.

Secondary wing feathers are the inner flight feathers. They have rounded tips and curved shafts, and in dabbling ducks, a colorful patch is found in the mid vane. These feathers are attached to the ulna bone. Numbers vary between 9 and 25, and these feathers give the bird lift while gliding.

Tertial feathers are the inner flight feathers (wing feathers closest to the body). These feathers are attached to the humerus bone and numbers vary between 3 and 4.

Speculum feathers are brightly colored secondary feathers.

Coverts feathers are feathers which cover other feathers. For example, a patch of covert feathers on the leading edge and underside of the wings may be used in bird identification.

Tail.
The tail feathers, or rectrices, are used for steering and braking while the bird is flying. Most birds will have 12 tail feathers and the length, shape, and color can be used for identification.

Legs and Feet.
Legs and feet can be identified in many ways. Some birds have tiny feet and legs. These feet may be adapted for holding on to a tree branch. Ducks and geese

have webbed feet, which are good for paddling through the water. Eagles have muscular feet with long talons, which are good for grasping and killing prey.

The color of the feet can also be used for identification. When looking at ducks, they seem to come in just about any color you can think of.

Beak shape.

Birds have many different shapes to their beaks, and each one is a clue to how they eat. A hummingbird has a long, narrow, straw-like beak. It's modified for drinking nectar from plants. A hawk has a short, strong, hooked beak that is good for tearing meat. Ducks have a broader, flatter beak, which is often used for sifting food from the muddy bottom. The point is that if you recognize different beak shapes and which birds have the type of beak you currently see, then you can narrow down your options.

Eyes.

The color of the eye or a color pattern around it are sometimes used in identification.

Color.

As we see with most birds, the females tend to be duller and more camouflaged than the males. When it comes to egg laying, being camouflaged on a nest provides an advantage. Males tend to be brighter and more colorful. Brighter colors make it more difficult to survive, so it's thought that females go for the brighter colored males because they must be smart to survive with such a disadvantage (no camouflage).

Sounds.

Bird groups can produce sounds similar to other birds or a sound that is unlike any other. We know that ducks quack, geese honk, and some birds chirp while others sing a song. Besides a call, some birds produce other distinct sounds. Woodpeckers produce a drumming sound as they make holes in trees. I can identify a mourning dove without even looking at it by the sound the wings make in flight. Pick up on these audio clues and use more than your eyes.

Habitat.

The environment in which a bird is found can be another good clue. Is the bird wading through a swamp? Is the bird in an open field walking about? Is the bird very high in the tallest tree in the area? This and more can give clues as to what bird we are seeing.

Behavior.
   Watching what the bird is doing can give us a clue about what the bird is, or at least what group it belongs to. Is the bird dabbling in the water like a duck? Is the bird hammering its beak into a tree like a woodpecker? Is the bird wading through the water while it snatches fish? Is the bird diving at smaller birds and tearing them to pieces? All of this and more can give us a great clue as to what the bird is.

Season.
   We all know that many birds migrate, but some don't. When seeing a bird, ask yourself which birds would be here at that time of year. For example, we only see many species of ducks in the winter, but other birds are found in our area year round.

Blue-Jay shown below.

Acadian Flycatcher (*Empidonax virescens*)

Rapid Identification – This is a small olive-green bird. The chest and belly are pale to a light olive (sometimes yellow), and the wings are dark with two white wing bars. Females are paler than males.

Sounds – The song is a rapid, two-syllable squeaky "cheep." It sounds a little like two rapid squeaks from a dog toy. It is sometimes described as a "ker-chip" sound. The males will produce a "peet-sah" song.

Diet – Insects and insect larvae are on the menu.

Season found in Texas – Spring and summer in the eastern ¼ of Texas.

American Crow (*Corvus brachyrhynchos*)

Rapid Identification – The American Crow is a large, all-black bird quickly identified by its size and noisy call. It's large size, no markings of any kind, and loud call set it apart from most birds. The male and female are practically identical in all ways. The black feathers will shine a bit in sunlight.

Sounds – The American Crow is often heard making the unique "caw-caw-caw" call. This call is loud and often made. Once you hear it, you know that nothing else sounds like it.

Diet – A crow will eat just about anything that is edible, and because they will eat carrion (dead things), most people won't eat a crow. Carrion feeders tend to carry disease, so you don't want to eat one. Now they will eat seeds, fruit, insects, eggs, fish, amphibians, reptiles, mammals, and just about anything else.

Season found in Texas – Year-round in the eastern half.

American Goldfinch (*Spinus tristis*)

Rapid Identification – A very small, bright, canary-yellow finch with a large black patch on the forehead and black wings. Females are a duller yellow-green color and lack the black spot on the forehead.

Sounds – The calls are a series of rapid, high-pitched chirps and whistles. Many different calls have been identified. There are rapid calls, an alarm call, more nasal sounding calls, flight calls, flock calls, and more.

There is a flight call this bird is known for. Some think they hear the birds saying "po-ta-to-chip" at this time.

Diet – This bird eats mostly seeds but will take a few small insects.

Season found in Texas – Fall and winter in all parts of Texas.

American Kestrel (*Falco sparverius*)

Rapid Identification – This small falcon has a head with brown, gray, white, and two black vertical lines on the face. The back is rust brown with black bars, and the tail is rust brown with a black tip. The chest has a light rust color, and the belly is white with black spots. The wings are blue-gray (slate) above, and below, they are white with black bars. This falcon is about the size of a mourning dove.

Sounds – The most common call is a loud "killy" sound repeated for a second or two.

Diet – The diet consists mostly of insects, bats, reptiles, frogs, birds, and rodents.

Season found in Texas – The American Kestrel can be found year-round in the northern half of Texas, but only in the fall and winter in the southern half.

American Pipit (*Anthus rubescens*)

Rapid Identification – A small bird with a yellow to cinnamon chest and belly with dark streaks. From above, the bird is gray with black streaks. Most of the tail is black, but the lateral feathers are white. The eye is black with a white eye ring and eyebrow stripe. The head and bill are small. This bird likes wet areas and will be seen walking instead of hopping and bobbing its tail.

Sounds – The common call is a rapid series of three "pi-pit" sounds. Songs are a cheerful "chwee" call repeated over and over.

Diet – Insects, insect larvae, spiders, crustaceans, and some plant matter are eaten.

Season found in Texas – Central and southern Texas will see them in the winter months. Northern Texas may only see them as they migrate through the area.

American Redstart (*Setophaga ruticilla*)

Male   Female

Rapid Identification – For males, the top of the bird is mostly black. The head, neck, throat, back, much of the wings, and tail tips are black, but the rump is white. There is bright orange on their sides in front of each wing, orange wing bars, and orange on the tail. The tip of the tail has a wide black band. For females, the top of the bird is mostly gray. The head, neck, back, and most of the wings are gray. Some of the wings and tail tips are black, but the rump is white.

Sounds – 5 or 6 high-pitched notes are sung in rapid succession, with the last note being shorter than the previous ones. The song is soft and musical.

Diet – Insects including moths, flies, wasps, beetles, and spiders. Some seeds and berries are consumed.

Season found in Texas – Most of Texas is a migratory path for this bird. They may be seen in the spring and fall near the eastern border of the state.

American Robin (*Turdus migratorius*)

Rapid Identification – This bird is a large member of the thrush family. The large size, black head, bright red belly, and gray back, tail, and wings set it apart from other birds. The female is not as brightly colored as the male.

Sounds – The song of the American Robin is associated with the arrival of spring, as this songbird is common at that time and loves to proclaim its territory. Singing generally begins in March, as males attract females. They enjoy calling in the early morning, so this is often when they are heard.

The songs are compared to a string of cheery chirps, and there is often a pause after every few notes.

Diet – Earthworms are a common food item, so the robin is often seen plucking them from the soil. They also enjoy insects, and they are often seen chasing them across the ground. Berries are consumed more in the cold winter months.

Season found in Texas – Year-round in most of Texas. Wintertime for the southwest region.

American Tree Sparrow (*Spizelloides arborea*)

Rapid Identification – A round-bodied sparrow with a rusty cap and rusty eyeline on a gray face. The short bill is black above and yellow below. From below, the bird is white with a black spot in the center of the breast. From above, the back is rusty, and the wings have two white stripes. The tail is long, thin, and dark.

Sounds – Males sing a 1-2 second song of high-pitched notes that fall near the end. When feeding, they produce a musical "teedle-eet."

Diet – They will eat grasses, berries, insects, seeds, and insect larvae.

Season found in Texas – North Texas will see this bird in the winter months.

Ash-throated Flycatcher (*Myiarchus cinerascens*)

Rapid Identification – From below, the throat, neck, and chest are white, but the belly is lemon yellow. From above, the back is gray, and the wings are brown with white stripes. The long tail is brown above and cinnamon below. The face is gray, and the crown is tall, ridged, and often darker than the rest of the bird. The overall body shape is long and slender.

Sounds – Males sing a gurgling song early in the morning. Songs later in the day are more of a sputtering whistle. Other calls consist of trills, "br-ick", and "urg."

Diet – Spiders, insects, wasps, bees, bugs, flies, caterpillars, and larvae.

Season found in Texas – West and central Texas will see them in the spring and summer.

Baltimore Oriole (*Icterus galbula*)

Rapid Identification – Males have a black head, neck, wings, and back. The chest and belly are bright orange. The tail is orange below and black on top, with an orange tip and borders. The female will have a brown to yellow head, neck, chest, belly, and tail with dark wings. Males and females have two white bars on the wings.

Sounds – The male sings paired notes that sound clear and flute-like. Rapid chattering and slow whistles may also be made.

Female and Male

Diet – Ripe fruit, nectar, and insects.

Season found in Texas – The Baltimore Oriole migrates through most of Texas, but not the western ¼ of the state.

Bank Swallow (*Riparia riparia*)

Rapid Identification – This small, fast-flying bird has a little head that is mostly dark with a white chin and neck. The bill is very short and small. The upper part of the chest has a dark ring and a thin line running down the sternum. The top of the bird is gray to brown, and from below, the bird is white. The wings are dark above and below. The tail is dark above, white below, and has a tiny fork.

Sounds – Males produce a rapid, bubbling chatter. The call in flight is a fast, guttural "tschr tschr."

Diet – Insects such as bees, wasps, butterflies, and moths are caught in flight. Ants will also be eaten.

Season found in Texas – Most of Texas will only see this bird as it's migrating through. There is a breeding group found in southern Texas.

Barn Owl (*Tyto alba*)

Rapid Identification – A unique bird with a white, heart-shaped face. The top of the head, back of the neck, back, wings, and tail are a cinnamon brown irregularly spotted with gray. The throat, chest, and belly are mostly white, with some tan areas and small black spots. The legs are long and white, but the feet are colored like the wings. Females tend to be darker where dark spots and bars are found. The dark spots and bars are present but less obvious on the males.

Sounds – Barn owls make a horrible scream or screech when they are vocal. They are also known for snapping their bills together when angry or afraid.

Diet – Mostly small rodents, but some birds, lizards, and other small prey may be taken.

Season found in Texas – Year round.

Barn Swallow (*Hirundo rustica*)

Rapid Identification – A small bird that is bright metallic blue on top and rusty on bottom. The back of the head and neck are metallic blue, while the front is rusty brown. The chest and belly look white with a light rusty stain. The tail is deeply forked and has a bold white bar across it. The female is very similar in appearance but, like many species, not as bright as the male.

Sounds – The calls are made often and sound like a rapid twittering or warble. A random buzzing sound is mixed in with the others.

Diet – Flying insects make up most of the barn swallow's diet, and the insects will be taken mostly from the air. Small amounts of seeds and berries will be eaten.

Season found in Texas – Spring and summer. Breeding season.

Barred Owl (*Strix varia*)

Rapid Identification – A large brown and white (gray) bird with a round face and yellow beak. The chest and belly have vertical brown streaks (bars) running all the way down to the tail. The back, wings, and tail are brown and white with horizontal bars. The owl gets its name because it's covered in bars front and back. The male and female look alike, but the female is 1/3 larger than the male. She may need this additional size and weight due to what she loses while incubating the eggs.

Sounds – This bird has a very well-known call. If you have ever heard an owl, it was probably this one. It sounds like the bird is saying, "Who cooks for you?" or "hoo-hoo-hoo-hoo, hoo-hoo-hoo-hoo."

Diet – Rodents, birds, amphibians, reptiles, crustaceans, and fish make up the diet of the barred owl.

Season found in Texas – Year-round in the eastern half of Texas.

Bell's Vireo (*Vireo bellii*)

Rapid Identification – The gray head has a pale white broken eye ring and a thin dark line through each eye. The bill is short, thick, and pale. The back is gray to light yellow, and the wings are dark with two white wingbars. The belly is white to pale yellow, and yellow may only be seen on the flanks. The tail is long, thin, and dark. Eastern specimens will have much more yellow.

Sounds – The song is a loud, rapid "cheedle cheedle chee." Calls are noisy, angry, and wren-like.

Diet – Insects, spiders, and small berries will be eaten.

Season found in Texas – Much of Texas, except for the northwest and southeastern regions, may see this bird in the spring and summer. Watch for them in dense brush and young forests.

Bewick's Wren (*Thryomanes bewickii*)

Rapid Identification – A small, round bird that is brown above and pale below. The beak is long, thin, dark, and slightly curved. The head is brown above, with a white eyebrow stripe and a white chin. The belly is pale and often has brown streaks. The back and wings are brown, and dark bars are seen on the wings. The tail is long, covered in dark bars, often held up, and flicked about.

Sounds – Males sing many songs. The most common is a rapid warble, ending with a high-pitched trill. The song is short and only lasts about two seconds.

Diet – Insects, spiders, larvae, insect eggs, and some plants and seeds.

Season found in Texas – Year-round in all parts of Texas.

Black-and-white Warbler (*Mniotilta varia*)

Rapid Identification – A small bird with black and white stripes over its entire body. This is one of the easiest birds to identify. The male and female do have a few differences. The male has a large black patch over the ear area, but the female has a thin black line (eyeline). The male also has a black throat, but the female has a white one. Lastly, the female has more white over her body than the male.

Sounds – The song is described as squeaky and compared to the sound of a small, squeaky wheel being turned. May be described as a "weezy-weezy-weezy" sound.

Male
Black patch behind eye and black throat.

Female
Black eyeline and white throat.

Diet – Insects.

Season found in Texas – Spring and summer in the northeastern ¼. Migration only in most other parts of the state. Fall and winter in the southeastern region.

Black-capped Vireo (*Vireo atricapilla*)

Rapid Identification – Males are recognized by their black heads and white patches (spectacles) around their red eyes. There is a white patch in front of the eyes and a white chin. Females have a gray head. The chest and belly are white, while the flanks are yellow. The back is yellow at the top and black lower down, with two white stripes when the bird is perched. The wings have two yellow bars with a black bar between them. Females are duller than males. The legs and toes are dark, long, and thin.

Sounds – The males sing rapid twittering notes that rise and fall in tone.

Diet – Insects, insect larvae, spiders, and some plants are eaten. They will take prey from the air at times, but mostly they will pluck them from trees and bushes.

Season found in Texas – This bird is seen more in central Texas.

Black-chinned Hummingbird
(*Archilochus alexandri*)

Rapid Identification – Males have black heads, a long black bill, a tiny white spot behind each eye, a white neck, and purple under the chin. The purple may only be seen in the right light. Adult males have a dark body with some metallic green on their backs. From below, the tail is dark with white tips on the three outer tail feathers. Females have metallic green backs, are white below, and have gray to green heads.

Sounds – Calls sound like rapid peeps and warbles. One display call sounds like a buzzing cricket.

Diet – Most of the diet will be nectar taken from flowers, but tiny insects are sometimes eaten.

Season found in Texas – This tiny bird is found mostly in the central, southern, and western parts of Texas.

Black-crested Titmouse (*Baeolophus atricristatus*)

Rapid Identification – A small bird with a gray face and a tall black crest running above the white forehead up to a point. The eyes are large and black, and the bill is short, thick, and black. The belly is gray to white, and the flanks have a flash of peach. The back, wings, and tail are a darker gray than the rest of the bird.

Sounds – The song is a high-pitched "peter-peter-peter."

Diet – They will eat insects such as flies, moths, beetles, and larvae. Other foods, like berries and seeds, are also taken.

Season found in Texas – This bird is absent in the eastern half of Texas and the northwestern region. Other parts of Texas may see them year-round.

Black-headed Grosbeak
(*Pheucticus melanocephalus*)

Rapid Identification – Males have black heads with a little orange running from behind the head to the rear of each eye. The neck, chest, and belly are orange. The wings and tail are black with white patches. Yellow may be seen under the wings or on the belly. The bill is thick and conical. Females and immature birds are lighter than males, have some streaking on the belly, and have white stripes on top of the head and above each eye.

Sounds – The song is a soft warble similar to a robin.

Diet – Seeds, insects, spiders, and fruits are all eaten.

Season found in Texas – This bird can be seen migrating across central and western Texas.

Black-tailed Gnatcatcher (*Polioptila melanura*)

Rapid Identification – This is a small, mostly gray bird with a large tail. Breeding males will have a black cap, while nonbreeding males will have a black spot above each eye. Females have a gray head with no black. The bill is tiny, black, and sharp-tipped. From below, males and females are white. The wings are short and dark, with a few white stripes. The tail is long, black, wide when spread out, and has white spots on the outer edges.

Sounds – The song is a rapid, three or four note "chee-chee-chee-chee" followed by a scolding buzz.

Diet – They eat insects, fruits, and seeds.

Season found in Texas – The southwestern edges of Texas may see this bird year round.

Black-throated Sparrow
(*Amphispiza bilineata*)

Rapid Identification – The top of the head and cheeks are gray with a long, white stripe above each eye and a second white stripe running from the bottom of the bill to the neck. A thin, white crescent is seen beneath each eye. The throat has a large, triangular, black patch. Juveniles are paler and lack the black throat patch. Its back is brown, and the belly is white. The tail is long, thin, and black, with white tips on the lateral feathers.

Sounds – Songs are two notes followed by a trill. Calls are a high-pitched "tink."

Diet – They eat insects and seeds.

Season found in Texas – This bird can be found year-round in central and southwestern Texas.

Blue-gray Gnatcatcher
(*Polioptila caerulea*)

Rapid Identification – This tiny bird is blue-gray above and white below. Breeding males have a black line above each eye that meets at the front of the head. A white eye ring surrounds both eyes, and the bill is tiny, thin, and sharp. The wings are dark with one white stripe. The tail is long and black, with white outer tail feathers.

Sounds – The call is a whining buzz, and the song is a series of short whistles.

Diet – This bird eats spiders and insects.

Season found in Texas – This bird can be found year-round along the southern border of Texas. The other parts of the state will see it in the spring and summer.

Blue Grosbeak (*Passerina caerulea*)

Rapid Identification – The male is a bright blue bird with two chestnut bars on the wings, and the lower half of the bill is silver. The female is a light cinnamon brown with two brown wingbars.

Sounds – The songs are described as a jumbled or musical warble lasting only a few seconds. Calls sound like a metallic clink.

Male   Female

Diet – Insects like grasshoppers, cicadas, and praying mantises are taken along with many others. They will also eat spiders, snails, seeds, and grains.

Season found in Texas – Spring and summer throughout Texas.

44

Blue-headed Vireo (Vireo solitarius)

Rapid Identification – The head is blue-gray, and each eye has a white eye ring and a black line running from the front of each eye to the bill. A white line runs from the front of each eye and meets above the bill. The bottom of the bird is white, and the flanks are yellow. The back can be gray or yellow, and the wings are black with two white wing bars separated by black. The tail is short, thin, black with some yellow, and has a small fork.

Sounds – The song is a combination of two syllables, two more, and then three. They are described as saying, "Hear me, see me, here I am."

Diet – Insects, insect larvae, spiders, snails, and fruit are eaten.

Season found in Texas – South Texas will see this bird in the fall and winter. Most other parts will see it as it migrates through.

Blue Jay (*Cyanocitta cristata*)

Rapid Identification – A large, bright blue bird that is blue on top and white on bottom. The blue head crest and black necklace make for rapid identification. Male and female blue jays look alike, so the only way to tell them apart is by behavior. The trailing edges of the wings and tail tips are white.

Sounds – Their call is often described as a loud, two-syllable "jay, jay" call. One of their calls sounds very much like a Red-shouldered Hawk or Red-tailed Hawk. Perhaps they make this sound to scare away other birds.

Diet – Seeds make up most of the Blue Jay diet, but they will eat just about anything edible. They are known to consume other birds, small animals, insects, and eggs.

Season found in Texas – Year-round in most of Texas. They are scarce in the southwest region.

Brewer's Blackbird
(*Euphagus cyanocephalus*)

Rapid Identification – Males appear black sometimes, and in the right sunlight, they may be a combination of shiny black, purple, and green. The eyes are bright yellow with a black pupil. Females are brown, a little darker on the wings and tail, and usually lack yellow eyes. Some may have a little of the color seen in males.

Sounds – Calls are a rapid "chuk chuk," and songs are a metallic "squee."

Diet – Most of the diet will be seeds and grains, but insects are taken during the warmer months. In cities, they will eat almost anything.

Season found in Texas – All of Texas can see this bird in the fall and winter.

Brewer's Sparrow (*Spizella breweri*)

Rapid Identification – This little bird is a bit plain. From above, they are brown with black marks on the back and wings. From below, they are gray and sometimes have dark vertical strikes on the chest and belly. The head is a bit large, the bill is short, a dark stripe is seen behind each eye, and the top of the head is darker than the rest. The tail is long and thin. This bird is sometimes known as "the bird without a field mark."

Sounds – The song is a trill followed by many different musical notes.

Diet – Small insects, spiders, and seeds are eaten.

Season found in Texas – West Texas may see this sparrow as it migrates through their area. The far western part of the state may see them in the fall and winter.

Broad-winged Hawk (*Buteo platypterus*)

Rapid Identification – A small hawk with a light brown head, neck, and chest mottled with white. The back and wings are a darker brown than the front. The chest and belly are white with brown horizontal bars. The wings are broader than those seen on most raptors. The underside of the wings is banded near the trailing edge, the wing lining is tan, and a very noticeable dark band is found on the trailing edge. The tail is strongly banded in brown and white, with the tail tip having a broad white band followed by a broad brown band.

Sounds – The call of the Broad-winged Hawk is a surprisingly high-pitched whistle. The female's call is slightly lower than that of the male.

Diet – Small mammals, birds, reptiles, amphibians, and insects are eaten.

Season found in Texas – East Texas may see them as they migrate through.

Bronzed Cowbird (*Molothrus aeneus*)

Rapid Identification – Males are black with dark blue wings and tails. Like some other birds, the bright colors may only appear in the right light. Males are known for fluffing up the feathers around their necks. Females are dark brown and plain. Males and females are known for their bright red eyes.

Sounds – High pitched whistles, squeaks, and squeals are produced.

Diet – Insects, seeds, and perhaps ticks off of livestock are eaten.

Season found in Texas – Southern Texas may see this bird in the spring and summer.

Brown Creeper (*Certhia americana*)

Rapid Identification – This tiny bird is often seen on large trees as it forages up and down them. The head is mottled in brown and white above; a white eyebrow streak is above each eye; and the bill is long, thin, and curved. From above, the bird is mottled in brown and white, with some black. From below, they are all white, and the tail is long and thin. The tail is often used as support as the bird moves up trees. A white stripe is seen across the wings when the bird is in flight.

Sounds – The song is a rapid, high-pitched "tsee." They are said to sing "tree, tree, beautiful tree."

Diet – Insects, insect larvae, spiders, and spider eggs are eaten.

Season found in Texas – This bird is found in Texas in the fall and winter.

Brown-crested Flycatcher
(Myiarchus tyrannulus)

Rapid Identification – The top of the head is brown and peaked. The lower half of the head is gray, and the bill is thick. The wings and tail are brown and black with white edges that make two wingbars. The primary feathers often have a little red on them. From below, the tail is light brown and almost red with dark edges. The chest is gray to white, and the belly is lemon yellow.

Sounds – The song is an unusual, trilled whistle. Calls are a short "whit."

Diet – Insects, spiders, lizards, and perhaps small hummingbirds are eaten.

Season found in Texas – The far south areas of Texas will see this bird in the spring and summer.

Brown-headed Cowbird (*Molothrus ater*)

Rapid Identification – The male is a small black bird with a brown head and neck. The body is black and a little shiny. The female's entire body is brown and maybe a little gray. Her wings are a little darker than her brown body.

Sounds – The call of the male is often described as a rapid, squeaky gurgle. They also use whistles and chatters. One call sounds like the constant dripping of water.

Notice the one odd colored egg above. That is the egg of a Brown-headed Cowbird in the nest of another bird species.

Diet – Grass seeds make up most of the bird's diet, but they will also take insects. They can be seen riding on the backs of animals like cows, and they probably do so to catch insects the cow scares up as it walks.

Season found in Texas – Year-round throughout Texas.

Brown-headed Nuthatch (*Sitta pusilla*)

Rapid Identification – A tiny bird with a large brown cap, a dark line through each eye (eye line), white cheeks and throat, a blue gray (slate) back, and a blue gray belly that is whiter than the back of the bird. The wings are blue gray (slate) close to the shoulders but browner towards the tips. The tail is blue gray (slate) and brown as you get closer to the tip. The male and female look alike. The female may be a little lighter in color than the male.

Sounds – The common call of this bird sounds just like someone is squeezing a tiny rubber dog toy. Often, they will call several times, pause, and repeat.

Diet – Insects, spiders, and pine seeds.

Season found in Texas – Year-round in the eastern region of Texas that is near Louisiana.

Brown Thrasher (*Toxostoma rufum*)

Rapid Identification – A large brown to reddish brown bird on top and a mostly white belly with dark streaks on the bottom. The streaks will sometimes look like spots. The wings have two thin black bars, with each bordered to the rear by a thin white bar. The legs and tail are both long. Males and females look alike.

Sounds – Brown Thrashers can sing an almost endless number of songs, but a short, loud smack is commonly heard. They seem to be complaining when using this call and often sing phrases in pairs. Listen for the same sound twice, and then a different sound twice, and so on.

Diet – The diet is mostly insects, but some seeds and fruit will be taken. Worms and the occasional small amphibian or reptile may also be eaten.

Season found in Texas – Year round in the eastern ¼ of Texas and wintertime in the eastern half.

Bullock's Oriole (*Icterus bullockii*)

Rapid Identification – The top of the head is black with an orange stripe below it. The eyes have a black line running through them, with orange below and a black throat. From below, all of the bird is orange. From above, the back and tail are black. The wings are black with a broad white stripe. The tail is orange below with a black tip and black above. Females are paler than males and usually lack the throat patch. The bill of each is sharp and pointed.

Sounds – Calls are a chatter, followed by a few whistles, and then a few "teers."

Diet – Insects, spiders, lizards, nectar, and fruit are eaten.

Season found in Texas – West and central Texas will see this bird in the spring and summer.

Bushtit
(Psaltriparus minimus)

Rapid Identification – This small bird is round, plain, and has a long tail. From above, they are gray to brown, and from below, they are gray to white. Some birds will have a light brown head, and others will be gray. The bill is dark and very short. Some birds in Texas, especially in the southern areas, have a black mask. Males have dark eyes, and females have pale eyes.

Sounds – Calls consist of rapid "chips" and "pits."

Diet – Insects, spiders, and a few seeds are eaten.

Season found in Texas – Parts of central and western Texas may see this bird year round.

Cactus Wren
(*Campylorhynchus brunneicapillus*)

Rapid Identification – The top of the head is brown with a white eyebrow streak below it. Behind each eye is a dark line, and the cheeks are pale with black dashes. The bill is long, thin, and slightly curved. The back is brown and speckled in black and white. The long, thin tail consists of many black bars with a little white in between them. The throat is dark, the chest is white, the belly is rusty, and both the chest and belly are covered in black spots, making vertical rows.

Sounds – The song is a repeating "chug-chug-chug-chug," that sounds like a car trying to start.

Diet – Insects, spiders, and fruit are eaten.

Season found in Texas – Central, southern, and west Texas can see this bird year round.

58

Canyon Towhee (*Melozone fusca*)

Rapid Identification – This sparrow has a rusty patch on top of its head and another under its tail. Most of the bird is gray with a little brown. The chest is white with a small black spot near the top of the sternum. The tail is long, and so are the legs.

Sounds – The song is described as a musical "chili chili chili."

Diet – Seeds, grasses, berries, spiders, and insects are eaten.

Season found in Texas – This bird can be seen year-round in central and western Texas.

Canyon Wren (*Catherpes mexicanus*)

Rapid Identification – The top of the head and back are mottled in black, white, and reddish brown. The bill is long and thin, and the eyes are small and black. The throat and chest are white, while the belly is reddish brown with black spots. The tail is reddish brown with thin black bars. The wings are the same color as the body and have thin black bars.

Sounds – The song is a loud series of notes that descend and slow as it finishes.

Diet – Insects and spiders are eaten and sometimes taken from spiderwebs.

Season found in Texas – This bird can be seen year-round in west and central Texas.

Carolina Chickadee (*Poecile carolinensis*)

Rapid Identification – A tiny bird with a black head, broad white cheeks, a black throat, a white and tan chest and belly, a gray back, and wings with thin white stripes. Watch for them to be hanging upside down on branches as if they are putting on a show. There are no clear anatomical differences between males and females.

Sounds – The Carolina Chickadee has a characteristic four-note whistle. There will be a high, low, high, low, pitch note rhythm to the call. It may sound like "see-day-see-day." They will repeat this four-note whistle over and over in the spring.

Diet – Seeds, berries, caterpillars, insects, and spiders make up their diet.

Season found in Texas – Year-round in the eastern half of Texas.

Carolina Wren (*Thryothorus ludovicianus*)

Rapid Identification – A tiny bird with a brown head, back, wings, and tail. The wings and tail have thin black bars running across them. This bird has a distinct white stripe above each eye (eyebrow stripe). The cheeks and throat are white, while the chest and belly are tan. The male and female look the same.

Sounds – This little bird is unusually loud for its size, and even though its small size may make it difficult to spot in brush, its song will give away its location. Listen for a two-syllable whistle to be repeated five times. They are known for singing more than most birds and may sing thousands of times in a day. The sound is often described as "tweedle-tweedle-tweedle-tweedle-tweedle."

Diet – Insects and spiders are favorite foods. They will eat almost any small insect, but they will also take small lizards, frogs, and maybe snakes. Seeds and fruits will also be eaten.

Season found in Texas – Year-round in the eastern 2/3 of Texas.

Cassin's Sparrow (*Peucaea cassinii*)

Rapid Identification – The top of the head is dark, and a black eyeline is seen behind each eye. A faint eye ring is sometimes seen. The face is pale, and so is the cone-shaped bill. The back of the bird is a mix of brown and black, with white edges on the feathers. The chest and belly are pale, with some dark streaks.

Sounds – The song begins with two whistling notes, followed by a trill and two more notes.

Diet – Seeds, insects, and spiders are eaten.

Season found in Texas – All but the eastern part of Texas can find this bird year round.

Cedar Waxwing (*Bombycilla cedrorum*)

Rapid Identification – A medium-sized bird with a light brown (peach) head, neck, and chest. An obvious crest and a black mask with white borders are seen on the face. The belly is a light yellow. The back and wings are mostly gray. The wings have red wax-like tips on the secondary feathers, and the tail has a bright yellow bar at the tip. Males and females look alike.

Sounds – Most often, a very high-pitched rapid trilling sound is made, and there are three syllables in the call. A "whistle-trill-whistle" song is heard.

Diet – Cedar berries are a favorite food of this bird. Insects will be taken during the warmer months, but this bird eats mostly fruits. From fall into winter, they may be seen eating juniper and mistletoe. The birds are sometimes seen eating sap.

Season found in Texas – Fall and winter. Nonbreeding season.

Chestnut-collared Longspur (*Calcarius ornatus*)

Rapid Identification – Breeding males have a black cap, a white eyebrow line, a black line behind each eye, light rust on the cheeks and chin, and a bright rust patch on the back of the neck. The chest and belly are black. The back is a mottling of black and brown with white edges on the feathers. The tail is black down the center, but the outer edges are white. Nonbreeding birds are brown with dark streaks above. Below, they are gray with some streaks.

Sounds – The song is a mix of warbles and gurgling pitches.

Diet – Insects and seeds are eaten.

Season found in Texas – North and west Texas will see them in the fall and winter.

Chihuahuan Raven (*Corvus cryptoleucus*)

Rapid Identification – A large black bird with a stout bill that has feathers covering part of it. The area just below the neck may have a small patch of white feathers. In flight, the first six primary feathers separate from the others and are fingerlike in appearance. This bird is also known as the White-necked Raven.

Sounds – The call sounds like a "caw" or a "kraak." It is similar in sound to the American crow but lower in pitch.

Diet – Like other birds in the crow family, this bird will eat just about anything. They often walk on the ground, looking for anything edible. This will include grains, insects, worms, spiders, fish, amphibians, reptiles, birds, and mammals.

Season found in Texas – The western half of Texas can see this bird year-round.

66

Chimney Swift
(*Chaetura pelagica*)

Rapid Identification – A small gray or brown torpedo shaped bird with long, narrow, sweeping wings, and a very short tail. Males and females look alike.

Sounds – A rapid chattering call is heard while the bird is in flight. They are quite noisy and seem to try to attract attention to themselves.

Diet – Flying insects.

Season found in Texas – Spring and summer in all but the far western region of Texas.

Interesting Facts – The Chimney Swift is nicknamed "the cigar with wings" due to its torpedo shape.
Thousands of individuals may nest in one large chimney of an abandoned factory.

A Chimney Swift without a mate will sometimes help a mated pair raise young.

Chipping Sparrow (*Spizella passerine*)

Rapid Identification – A tiny bird with a reddish brown cap (crown), a black line through the eye (eyeline), and a plain gray belly. The wings are brown with black streaks and two thin white wing bars. Males and females look alike. Look for the red cap for fast identification.

Sounds – A common song sounds like a rapid, high-pitched musical trill, which is often compared to the spinning of a machine. Quiet chip sounds are often made as they move about.

Diet – Grass seeds are the primary food item of this sparrow. Like many birds, they will eat more insects during the breeding season. They have been seen eating fruits.

Season found in Texas – Spring and summer in most of Texas. Only migrating birds are seen in the panhandle.

Clay-colored Sparrow (*Spizella pallida*)

Rapid Identification – This little sparrow has a brown line of feathers down the center of its head, followed by a white eyebrow stripe. Behind each eye is a thin brown stripe with tan below. A pale gray collar is a good field mark for this bird. The back is tan with black streaks and white edges on the feathers. The chest and belly are light tan to white. The bill is small, pale, and the same color as the legs. The tail is long, thin, and has a small notch at the end.

Sounds – The call will be 2-8 buzzes that sound like an insect.

Diet – Seeds, insects, and spiders.

Season found in Texas – Most of Texas will see this bird as it migrates through. To the far south and west, they may see it in the fall and winter.

Cliff Swallow
(*Petrochelidon pyrrhonota*)

Rapid Identification – The forehead has a distinct white patch, the top of the head is blue, and the rest of the face is cinnamon. The bill is tiny, and the back of the neck is white. The chest is dark to metallic blue, depending on the light, and the belly is white. The back is white, but there is a small white patch in the center of it. The wings and tail are dark, and a cinnamon patch is seen above the tail. The cave swallow (P. fulva) has a paler face and a darker rump.

Sounds – The song is an irritating, squeaky chatter. The call is a squeaky "chur."

Diet – Their diet consists of flying insects.

Season found in Texas – Most of Texas will see this bird in the spring and summer. The eastern region may only see them migrate through.

Common Ground Dove (*Columbina passerina*)

Rapid Identification – This small dove is pinkish brown on the front and brown with black spots on the back. The top and back of the head are gray, while the pale face, front of the neck, and sides of the neck are a light pink. The chest is light pink with brown spots, and the belly is light pink with fewer spots. The neck and chest have an unusual pattern that makes these areas look scaly. The back, wings, and tail are brown, and the wings have scattered black spots. The legs and feet are pink, and the area of the beak closest to the face is pink, while the tip of the beak is black. The underside of the wings is chestnut (cinnamon), and the brown tail has white corners.

Sounds – The wings make a fluttering sound when the bird takes to the air, and this dove has a higher pitched "coo" than what you usually hear with Mourning Doves. Common Ground Doves will produce a dozen or so of these rising coos and repeat them 4 or 5 times.

Diet – Seeds, grains, berries, and insects are commonly consumed.

Season found in Texas – The southern half of Texas can see this bird year-round.

Common Grackle (*Quiscalus quiscula*)

Rapid Identification – A medium sized black bird with a blue head. The head can look black depending on how the light hits it. The body and head can have an iridescent metallic look, and the feathers can reflect any color (often bronze) depending on how the light strikes the bird. Just look for a tall, very shiny blackbird with a blue to black head. The female is not as shiny, and they are often a browner color.

Sounds – Their most common call sounds like the rusty squeak of metal. When calling, they like to lift up the wings slightly, raise the tail, and puff out their feathers. A squeaky "readle-eak" sound is often made. They tend to be noisy birds.

Diet – Common Grackles will eat just about anything edible. Insects, spiders, worms, crustaceans, fish, amphibians, rodents, birds, and even bats are eaten. In the winter, seeds are the most commonly consumed item. Corn, rice, acorns, and sunflower seeds are favored. They will even eat garbage.

Season found in Texas – Year-round in most of Texas. Absent in the southwest portion of the state.

Common Raven (*Corvus corax*)

Rapid Identification – The raven is a large black bird with a thick, heavy bill that has feathers extending half way down the top portion. The raven is larger than a crow, and in flight, a wedge-shaped tail is seen. The neck is thick with feathers and is easily seen when the bird moves its head forward when calling. Juveniles are a duller brown, especially on the head and neck.

Sounds – The call is a low, gurgling croak or a two-syllable "wonk wonk."

Diet – Like other birds in the crow family, this bird will eat just about anything. They often walk on the ground, looking for anything edible. This will include grains, insects, worms, spiders, fish, amphibians, reptiles, birds, and mammals.

Season found in Texas – Year-round in west Texas.

Common Yellowthroat (*Geothlypis trichas*)

Rapid Identification – For the male, the top of the head (crown) and back of the neck are mottled black and yellow, with a white band beneath it (just above the eyes). There is a broad black mask over the face. The throat, chest, and belly are bright yellow. The flanks are duller. The wings and tail are a dark yellow. Look for a yellow bandit. The female lacks the broad black mask and the white band above it. This gives the female a light brown head, but she still has the yellow throat and belly.

Sounds – The most common call is a rapid, high-pitched sound described as "witchety-witchety-witchety." A fast "chip" sound may be heard.

Male | Female

Diet – This bird has a diet that is almost entirely insect based, but spiders are also taken. Some fruit and seeds will be eaten when insects aren't available.

Season found in Texas – Spring and summer in the eastern ¼ of the state. Migration only in the rest of Texas.

Cooper's Hawk (*Accipiter cooperii*)

Rapid Identification – A large bird but somewhat smaller than some hawks, like the red-tailed. The top of the head (crown) is blue gray (dark), and the same color is seen on the back, wings, and tail. The chest and belly are white with many rusty brown bars. Look for the dark cap on this hawk. The wings and tail have broad, dark bars. Females are larger and heavier, and the feathers are a little browner.

Sounds – These birds aren't as vocal as other hawks and make a repeated "cak-cak-cak" or "gik-gik-gik" call.

2 pictures of flying Cooper's Hawks.

Diet – Smaller birds make up most of the diet, but rodents and bats will also be taken.

Season found in Texas – Year-round in all but the southernmost edges of Texas. They are found in fall and winter in those southernmost areas.

Couch's Kingbird (*Tyrannus couchii*)

Rapid Identification – This flycatcher has a gray head, a small dark spot behind each eye, a white throat, and a thick bill. The chest, belly, and area under the tail are lemon yellow. The back is dark yellow, and the wings are black with white edges. The tail is long, dark, and notched.

Sounds – The call begins with several pairs of squeaks followed by a "tzeeeerr."

Diet – Flying insects and fruits are eaten.

Season found in Texas – Southern Texas can see this bird year-round.

Crested Caracara (*Caracara plancus*)

Rapid Identification – A very odd looking falcon with a flat dark head, large orange and blue bill, orange face, white cheeks and upper neck, black and white barred chest and upper back, black to brown body and wings, and long yellow to orange legs.

Sounds – The only sound this bird will make is a rattle, and often the only time that is heard is when they are annoyed. The rattling sounds like someone is dragging a stick along a fence. They will sometimes toss their heads back when making the rattle call.

Diet – The Crested Caracara won't hesitate to eat carrion and will chase off vultures to do so. Outside of carrion, they will also eat fish, reptiles, amphibians, birds, and mammals. They will watch for feeding vultures and dine beside them. They will also eat insects and dig up turtle eggs.

Season found in Texas– Year-round in in the central and southern parts of the state.

Curve-billed Thrasher (*Toxostoma curvirostre*)

Rapid Identification – The head is small and, like the rest of the bird, gray to grayish brown. The head also has bright yellow eyes and a long, black, curving bill. The throat is white, and the belly is white with dark spots. The area under the tail has a light rusty color, and the wings often have one thin white wing stripe. The very similar Crissal Thrasher (T. crissale) lacks spots on the belly.

Sounds – The song is a series of pleasant musical notes, and the call is a rapid double whistle that sounds like "whit-wheet."

Diet – Insects, spiders, snails, seeds, and fruits are eaten.

Season found in Texas – North, west, south, and central Texas may see this bird year-round.

Dark-eyed Junco (*Junco hyemalis*)

Rapid Identification – The light gray (slate) color variation of this sparrow is the most likely color to be seen in Louisiana. For males, the head, neck, chest, back, wings, and tail are a light gray (slate) color. The belly and underside of the tail are white. Females are more of a brown to gray mix, but overall, much browner.

Sounds – The males sing a rapid musical trill. The trill is consistently the same for each syllable. Faint chips and peeps are made when calling.

Male   Female

Diet – Various grass seeds and insects are taken.

Season found in Texas – Winter only. Nonbreeding season.

Dickcissel (*Spiza americana*)

Rapid Identification – This small sparrow-like bird has a gray to brown head with a yellow eyebrow stripe and a second yellow stripe starting at the base of the bill and running down. Males have a large, V-shaped black patch on the throat, but females lack this patch. The chest is yellow, and the belly is white. Males have a bright rusty patch on the shoulders, but females have less rust in this area. The back is brown, with black streaks going down the back. The tail is dark and has a notch at the end.

Sounds – The call is a buzzy "dip-dip-zeer-zeer-zeer." Some people think its call sounds like "dick-dick-cissel," which is where its name comes from.

Diet – Insects and seeds are eaten.

Season found in Texas – Central and East Texas may see this bird in the spring and summer.

Downy Woodpecker (*Dryobates pubescens*)

Male   Female

Rapid Identification – A small woodpecker with a black and white striped head and a red spot to the rear of the head. The entire underside of the bird is white; the back is black with a white stripe down the center; and the wings are black with white spots forming bars. Females lack the red spot on the head.

Sounds – The drumming on the sides of trees and a short peep are the most common sounds made by these birds. The peep may stand alone, or there could be a rapid succession of them. No song will be heard from this bird, but they do make plenty of noise.

Diet – Primarily insects are found inside trees and plant galls. They will take some berries and grains.

Season found in Texas – Year-round in the eastern part of the state and the panhandle. Absent from all other regions.

Eastern Bluebird (*Sialia sialis*)

Rapid Identification – A small bird with a bright blue head, back, and wings. The throat, chest, and belly are a rusty brown. The female has much less blue and much more brown.

Sounds – The Eastern Bluebird produces a soft musical warble. The call is often described as "chir-ee." They won't call and sing as much as other backyard birds, but the occasional chirp or trill will be heard.

Diet – Insects and berries. They have been known to take small reptiles and amphibians.

Season found in Texas – Year-round in the eastern 2/3 of Texas. Fall and winter in the western region except for the extreme southwest of the state.

Eastern Kingbird (*Tyrannus tyrannus*)

Rapid Identification – A small to medium sized bird with a black head and face. The back, wings, and most of the tail are dark. The throat, chest, belly, and tip of the tail are a snowy white. The wing feathers are edged in white. Males and females look alike.

Sounds – The song is a series of nasally tweets. Calls are sometimes described as electric and metallic. The call is a bit like a rapid, high pitched buzz.

Diet – Flying insects. Berries later in the year.

Season found in Texas – Spring to summer in the eastern 2/3 of the state. Absent from the western part of Texas.

Some people say the Eastern Kingbird looks as if it's wearing a business suit.

The Eastern Kingbird can recognize the egg of a Brown-headed Cowbird in the nest and will toss it out.

Eastern Meadowlark (*Sturnella magna*)

Rapid Identification – Medium sized songbird with black stripes, along with white and yellow patches on the head. The back is a mottling of brown, black, and white. The throat and belly are bright yellow, and there is a large black band across the top of the chest (bib), making a V shape. Females are a little smaller and don't have as much color as the males.

Sounds – This bird's song sounds like it's coming from a flute. 3 to 5 whistles will be repeated, dropping in pitch, and taking about two seconds. The song can be described as someone saying, "see-you, see-yeeeer."

Diet – Mostly insects. Seeds and fruit are taken in the winter. Sunflower seeds and cracked corn will attract this bird to your feeders.

Season found in Texas – Year-round in the eastern half of Texas.

Eastern Phoebe (*Sayornis phoebe*)

Rapid Identification – A robust songbird that is grayish brown on the head, back, and wings, with the head being the darkest. The throat, chest, and belly are white, and there is a white ring around the neck, which does fade to the back side. The wing feathers have white borders, which form two thin white bars. Females are slightly smaller than males.

Sounds – The call of the eastern phoebe is a high, two syllable call. Many describe the call as sounding like "fee-bee" repeated over and over. It may sound like a whistle followed by a rapid trill. They also produce a rapid peeping sound.

Diet – Insects make up most of their diet, but berries are taken in the winter.

Season found in Texas – Year-round in northeast Texas. Fall and winter in the remainder of the state, except for the Panhandle region.

Eastern Screech-Owl (*Megascops asio*)

Rapid Identification – A small gray owl with short ear tufts, large yellow eyes, and dark vertical streaks on the chest and belly. They blend amazingly well with tree bark. Females are a little (one inch) taller than males.

Sounds – The song is a soft, eerie sound often compared to a wail, trill, or whinny. Calls can sound like a screech or a hoot. They are also known for clacking their bills when they are irritated.

Diet – Small animals such as mammals, birds, reptiles, amphibians, crawfish, insects, worms, and sometimes each other will be eaten.

Season found in Texas – Year-round in all but the western edge of Texas.

Migration and Range – The Eastern Screech Owl doesn't migrate and can be found in the eastern two thirds of the U.S.

Most forests near water and open areas will attract screech owls. The trees need to be old and large enough to have tree cavities for nesting. Trees located along a lake, stream, bayou, or similar body of water are favored.

Putting up a nest box may be the best way to attract this bird to a place where you can see it.

Eastern Towhee (*Pipilo erythrophthalmus*)

Male   Female

Rapid Identification – The male is a round bird (sparrow) with a black head, throat, back, wings, and tail. The belly is white, and the sides (flanks) are a rusty brown. There are white marks on the outer wing feathers, and the tail is tipped in white, except for the feathers in the center. The female will have brown feathers replacing the black ones on the male.

Sounds – One common sound is a rapid, three syllable call. "See-hir," followed by a rapid trill. A second common call sounds as if the bird is saying "drink-your-tee."

Diet – Insects, spiders, and snails will be eaten when the weather is warm, and the prey is available. During the winter months, they will consume seeds and berries. They may eat a small lizard or similar animal.

Season found in Texas – Scarce in the eastern 1/3 of the state.

The towhee's name comes from a description of one of the bird's calls. Some hear the bird call as "tow-hee."

Eastern Wood-Pewee (*Contopus virens*)

Rapid Identification – The head is gray to brown with a crest on top and a white throat and neck. The bill is dark on top and yellow on bottom. The chest and belly are white and plain. The back is gray to brown, with long, dark wings and two white wing bars. The tail is long, thin, and dark, with a small notch.

Sounds – The song is three syllables in length and sounds like "pee-a-weeee."

Diet – Flying insects and small amounts of vegetation, berries, and seeds are eaten.

Season found in Texas – Most of central and eastern Texas can see this bird in the spring and summer. Southern and coastal areas will see it migrating through.

Elf Owl (*Micrathene whitneyi*)

Rapid Identification – This tiny owl has a brown, gray, and red face. There are bright yellow eyes and distinct white eyebrows, but no ear tufts. The throat and belly are mottlings of brown, gray, red, and white. The back is darker and is similar to the head in color. The wings show one bold white stripe and a second, less noticeable white stripe. The tail is short, dark above, and pale below.

Sounds – The song is a series of high-pitched notes that are sometimes compared to the barking of a small dog. The call is a short "whirr."

Diet – Insects, spiders, lizards, snakes, and small rodents are eaten.

Season found in Texas – Small parts of western and southern Texas may see this owl near the border of Mexico.

Eurasian Collared-Dove (*Streptopelia decaocto*)

Rapid Identification – A large dove with a pale sandy body, a long squared off tail, a thin beak, and a black collar around the sides and back of the neck, but not the front.

Sounds – Like other doves, the wings make a characteristic slapping sound when the bird takes to the air. The dove coo is usually soft, three syllables long, and accented (longer and louder) on the second syllable. A loud mewing sound similar to that of a catbird is made when they are startled.

Diet – Grains such as sunflower, millet, wheat, and corn are preferred. Some berries, insects, and plants will be consumed in small amounts.

Season found in Texas – Year-round in the entire state.

European Starling (*Sturnus vulgaris*)

Rapid Identification – A black bird with an iridescence that reflects purple and green colors. In the fall and winter, they are heavily spotted (white) and not as iridescent. In spring and summer, they are mostly black, with some spots still appearing on the back. The females don't have as much of the shine seen in the feathers of the males.

Sounds – European Starlings are very good at mimicking other birds, so they will make just about any sound that a bird can make. Squeaks, whistles, trills, and the sounds of other birds are common. Some songs can go on for a minute or more.

Diet – These birds have a wider diet than most, but they prefer insects over seeds and fruits. They have been known to eat garbage if it's available.

Season found in Texas – Year-round in the entire state.

Evening Grosbeak (*Coccothraustes vespertinus*)

Male   Female

Rapid Identification – Males have a black head with a large yellow patch above the eyes and a large yellow bill. The front of the bird is all yellow, and the back is dark yellow at the top, followed by a large white patch on the wings, followed by black. The tail is black and has a notch at the end. Females are mostly gray with a small amount of yellow, and black and white on the wings.

Sounds – The song is a short musical trill. Calls sound like chirps.

Diet – Insects, insect larvae, seeds, fruits, and berries are eaten.

Season found in Texas – All but the southern parts of Texas may see this bird in the fall and winter.

Ferruginous Hawk (*Buteo regalis*)

Rapid Identification – This large hawk is mostly white from below, except for brown patches near the front of the wings and black tips on the trailing edge of each feather, especially the first six. Also, from below, the wings look broad, and black patches are found on the tertiary feathers near the body. From above, the hawk's back is chestnut brown with black streaks. From below, the tail is white with a little rust near the tip and a V seen at the base of the tail.

Sounds – The call is a loud "kraaaaa."

Dark morph shown above.

Diet – Rabbits, squirrels, prairie dogs, gophers, amphibians, reptiles, insects, and birds are all eaten.

Season found in Texas – Eastern and central Texas may see this bird in the winter.

Field Sparrow (*Spizella pusilla*)

Rapid Identification – The top of the head is rusty, and each eye has a rusty eyeline. The bill is pink, and the face is gray with thin white eye rings. The belly is gray, with some rust near the chest. The back is brown with black streaks and two white wing bars.

Sounds – The song begins with slow whistles that accelerate to the end. The speed of the whistling has been compared to the sound of a bouncing ball as it stops.

Diet – Seeds, spiders, insects, and snails are eaten.

Season found in Texas – Northeast Texas can see this bird year-round. The rest of Texas may see it in the fall and winter.

Fox Sparrow (*Passerella iliaca*)

Rapid Identification – The top of the head has a rusty streak, followed by gray above the eyes and rusty cheeks. The body is round, and the chest, belly, and flanks are streaked in a rusty color. The back is rusty, and the tail is often the reddest part of the bird. The wings show two thin white wing bars. The bill is yellow mixed with dark colors. Western variations are more brown than red.

Sounds – The song is a mix of whistles, trills, and churs.

Diet – Insects, spiders, seeds, fruits, and some plant material are eaten.

Season found in Texas – Texas may see this bird in the fall and winter.

Golden-cheeked Warbler
(*Setophaga chrysoparia*)

Rapid Identification – This rare warbler is difficult to spot but worth the wait. Males have a bright yellow face with a black stripe on top of the head, a thin black stripe in front of and behind each eye, and a black throat. The chest and belly are white, and the flanks have black streaks. The back and tail are black with some white, and the wings have two white wing bars.

The female has less black than the male and little to no black throat.

Sounds – The call is "zee zee zee buzz zeeep."

Diet – Insects, insect larvae, and spiders are eaten.

Season found in Texas – Central Texas may see this bird in the spring and summer.

Golden-crowned Kinglet (*Regulus satrapa*)

Rapid Identification – A small, round, gray to olive bird with a broad yellow or orange stripe down the crown of the head. The yellow-orange stripe is bordered on the front and on each side by black. The back is gray (olive), the belly is tan to white, the wings are short with black and yellow, and so is the tail. The female may lack the orange in the crown.

Sounds – The song is a series of high pitched peeps that increase in frequency for about three seconds and end with a warble. Two or three "tsee" sounds are made between male and female.

Diet – Insects are preferred, and what will be taken when the days are warmer. Seeds are taken in the winter months.

Season found in Texas – All of Texas may see this bird in the fall and winter.

Golden-fronted Woodpecker
Melanerpes aurifrons

Male   Female

Rapid Identification – Most of the head and front of the bird are all white, and the back is black with horizontal white stripes. Males have a red spot on top of the head, a small yellow spot above the bill, and a large yellow-orange spot on the back of the head and neck. Females lack the red spot on top of the head. Some birds may have yellow on the lower belly.

Sounds – The song is a repeating "churrrr." The call is a repeating "chuck."

Male   Female

Diet – Insects, insect larvae, spiders, fruits, and nuts are eaten.

Season found in Texas – This bird is absent from east and west Texas, but the remainder of the state may see them year-round.

Grasshopper Sparrow
(*Ammodramus savannarum*)

Rapid Identification – The top of the head has a thin light stripe with two dark stripes on each side. The face is a light tan, and in front of each eye is a short yellow stripe. The eyes have a thin, white eye ring, and a thin, dark line is behind each eye. The chest is pale to light tan, with some dark spots on the chest. The flanks and shoulders have a little yellow on them. The back is brown with dark streaks. The tail is brown like the back and has a small fork.

Sounds – The song is a soft "kip-kip-kip-zeeeee." The call is seeet.

Diet – Insects and spiders are eaten, and grasshoppers are their favorite food.

Season found in Texas – North Texas may see this bird in the spring and summer. South Texas may see this bird year-round.

Gray Catbird (*Dumetella carolinensis*)

Rapid Identification – A medium sized, plain, slate gray bird with a dark cap on top of its head (crown). The feathers under the tail (undertail coverts) are chestnut red. Males and females look the same.

Sounds – The Gray Catbird has a characteristic call that sounds like a kitten meowing repeatedly. Other calls are a combination of squeaks and whistles. They can copy the calls and sounds of other birds and put them all together.

Diet – Insects and berries.

Season found in Texas – Spring and summer in the eastern 1/3 of Texas and migration through the central half.

The Gray Catbird can sing a song lasting up to 10 minutes.
The Gray Catbird will destroy the eggs of cowbirds if found in their nests.

Gray Hawk (*Buteo plagiatus*)

Rapid Identification – The head, neck, and most of the body are gray, as their name states. The eyes are large and black, and the bill is short, yellow near the face, and black near the tip. The back is a darker gray than the head, and from below, the chest and belly are gray with horizontal black bars. The long tail is banded in black and white with white tips. From below, the wings are gray with a dark trailing edge. Juveniles have dark blotches on the chest and belly.

Sounds – The call is a long "hoo-fleeeer." Other calls may be a repeated whistle or "creeee."

Diet – Lizards are the main prey item, but they will also eat snakes, toads, birds, rodents, and a few insects.

Season found in Texas – Small parts of Texas far to the west and south may see this hawk.

101

Great-crested Flycatcher
(*Myiarchus crinitus*)

Rapid Identification – The top of the big head is crested and brown, but the face is grayer. The throat is gray, and the belly is lemon yellow. The back is brown, and the wings have two white wingbars and white stripes. The tail is brown above, but rusty orange below with brown edges.

Sounds – The dawn song consists of two short whistles and a trill. A second call consists of "wheeep-wheeep-wheep."

Diet – Insects, berries, fruits, and spiders.

Season found in Texas – Most of central and eastern Texas can see this bird in the spring and summer.

Greater Roadrunner
(*Geococcyx californianus*)

Rapid Identification – The greater roadrunner is a long and slender bird that can be almost two feet in length. The head has a tall, dark, brown, and black crest with tiny white spots that can be raised or flattened. Breeding birds may show blue and orange behind the eyes. The belly is gray below, but the rest of the bird is brown with black streaks. The tail is very long, as are the legs. This long legged member of the cuckoo family can run as fast as 20 mph. They can fly but prefer to run. The greater roadrunner has more streaks on the chest than the lesser roadrunner.

Sounds – Males may produce a cooing sound that is similar to a dove. The bird may also make grunts, clucks, barks, rattles, and growls.

Diet – Reptiles, amphibians, insects, scorpions, seeds, fruits, eggs, birds, and small mammals are eaten.

Season found in Texas – This bird can be seen all over Texas year-round.

Great Horned Owl (*Bubo virginianus*)

Rapid Identification – This is a large owl with tall ear tufts and a thick body. The overall color is a gray and black mottled appearance. The front of the bird is often whiter than the back, and the belly may show horizontal barring.

Females are a little larger than males; females incubate the eggs while the male brings her food; and the male has a slightly deeper sound when it calls.

Sounds – Two owls are often heard calling back and forth to each other. They have a well-known "hoo-hoo-hoo-hoo" call. The call sounds deep and can be heard over long distances. Some people can tell that the male's call is deeper than that of the female.

Diet – A wide variety of small to large prey will be eaten. They will eat frogs, lizards, mice, other birds of prey, many bird species, rabbits, skunks, snakes, and much more.

Season found in Texas – Year round throughout the state.

Great-tailed Grackle
(*Quiscalus mexicanus*)

Rapid Identification – This is a large, dark bird that may appear blue or purple in the right light (males only). The head is small, the bill is thick and strong, and the eyes are yellow. The tail is long and broad, and can be fanned out very wide. The large tail is a key characteristic of this bird. Females are dark brown to black, with the back being dark and the belly being brown. Females may also have a thin, black line through each eye.

Sounds – Songs may sound like shrieks, squeaks, or a repeating "ki-ki-ki." Calls are more of a cluck, click, squeal, and more.

Diet – Grains, fruits, insects, amphibians, reptiles, fish, eggs, birds, and mammals are eaten.

Season found in Texas – This bird can be found year-round across Texas.

Green Jay (*Cyanocorax yncas*)

Rapid Identification – The spectacular head of this bird is bright blue with a large black eye patch, black behind the cheeks, and a large black throat that is bib-like in shape. A small white patch may be seen between the eyes on the forehead. The back is green, and the belly is more yellow close to the center and often light green closer to the flanks. The tail is dark green above, yellow below, and black-tipped with a fork at the end.

Sounds – The call may be a noisy "shink-shink-shink," rattling, and more.

Diet – This bird will eat insects, seeds, fruit, spiders, lizards, frogs, eggs, and small birds.

Season found in Texas – The southernmost parts of Texas may see this bird year round.

106

Green Kingfisher (*Chloroceryle americana*)

Male   Female

Rapid Identification – This small bird has a huge bill, a metallic green, flat head, and a white neck. Males have a large rust patch on the chest and a white belly with a scattering of green spots. Females lack the rusty chest patch, but they have two green bands, one on the chest and one on the belly. The back and wings are green, and the wings are dark near the tips. The wings have a scattering of white spots that may form two thin white wing bars. The tail is green above and white below.

Sounds – The call is a clicking sound that sounds like pebbles being tapped against each other. There may also be a buzzing or clicking call.

Diet – Fish make up most of their diet, but shrimp and insects are also eaten.

Season found in Texas – South and central Texas may see this bird.

Green-tailed Towhee (*Pipilo chlorurus*)

Rapid Identification – The top of the head has a large, rusty crown that may be raised as a crest. The head is gray, the eyes are tiny, and the bill is short and thick. The throat is white, the chest is gray, and the belly is lighter. The wings and tail are greenish-yellow with dark shades and are a defining characteristic.

Sounds – The song is a mix of whistles, trills, and peeps. They also have a mewing call.

Diet – Seeds, berries, and insects are eaten.

Season found in Texas – Central, south, and west Texas may see this bird in the fall and winter.

Hairy Woodpecker (*Dryobates villosus*)

Male   Female

Rapid Identification – A medium sized woodpecker with alternating black and white bands on the head along with a red spot on the top/rear of the head (crown). The front of the bird is all white, and the wings are covered in white spots, which form several bars. The female lacks the red crown spot.

Sounds – The call is a short peep or a rattle. The drumming of their bills against trees will also be heard.

Diet – Insects. Wood boring beetle larvae make up a large part of their diet. Some fruit and seeds are taken.

Season found in Texas – Year round in the eastern 1/3 of Texas.

Harris's Hawk (*Parabuteo unicinctus*)

Rapid Identification – This is a large hawk with broad, deep wings. The head and neck are dark, but the bill is bright yellow near the face and dark out close to the sharp tip. The chest and belly are dark, but the belly may have a few scattered small white patches, especially if they are young. The area beneath the tail is white. The back is dark, as are most of the wings, but the wings have large reddish brown patches at the shoulders. From below, the front of each wing (marginal coverts) is brown, and the rest of the wings are dark. From above, the tail is mostly black with a white tip. From below, the tail is white near the body, then mostly dark, and then has a white tip. The legs are reddish brown near the body and yellow near the feet.

Sounds – The call is a raspy, shrill shriek.

Diet – Rabbits, squirrels, reptiles, and birds are all eaten.

Season found in Texas – The southern and western regions of Texas may see this bird year-round.

Harris's Sparrow (*Zonotrichia querula*)

Breeding adult show above.

Rapid Identification – Breeding adults have a gray head, black forehead, black face, black throat (black bib), and a light orange bill. Nonbreeding adults swap out the gray on the face for a light brown. The chest is white with black streaks, the belly is white, and the flanks are brown with black streaks. The back is brown with black streaks, and the long tail looks the same.

Sounds – The song is a series of 1-3 simple whistles. The call is a loud peep.

Immature bird shown above.

Diet – This sparrow eats seeds, insects, berries, and grasses.

Season found in Texas – North and central Texas may see this bird in the winter.

Hepatic Tanager (*Piranga flava*)

Male   Female

Rapid Identification – Males are a beautiful red bird, while the female is yellow. Males have a red head and neck with a gray cheek patch and a dark silver bill. The throat, chest, and belly of the male are all red, but the back and tail are a darker red. Females are yellow with a gray cheek and thin, dark eyeline. The female's back and tail are a darker yellow.

Sounds – The song is a series of short whistles lasting a few seconds. Calls are a singular "chup."

Male   Female

Diet – Insects, spiders, and berries are eaten.

Season found in Texas – The far western region of Texas may see this bird in the spring and summer.

Hermit Thrush (*Catharus guttatus*)

Rapid Identification – From above, this bird is brown with a rusty red tail but with less rust on the wings. From below, the bird is white with dark spots forming vertical rows. The spots are bolder near the neck and paler as you go down the belly. The bill is pink close to the face and black at the tip.

Sounds – The song begins with a high note followed by a two syllable whistle. There is a pause, and the whistle repeats.

Diet – Insects, amphibians, reptiles, fruit, and berries are eaten.

Season found in Texas – All of Texas may see this bird in the fall and winter.

Hooded Oriole (*Icterus cucullatus*)

Rapid Identification – Males are bright yellow to orange on the top of the head and much of the neck, but they have a large black patch on the throat that extends up to the eyes. The chest, belly, area under the tail, and top of the back are bright yellow to orange, but the wings are black with two white wing bars and white stripes. Females are pale yellow with gray backs and gray wings with two white wing bars and white stripes.

Sounds – Songs are a series of rapid whistles, warbles, and chatters.

Male   Female

Diet – Insects, spiders, fruit, and nectar are eaten.

Season found in Texas – The southern border of Texas can see this bird in the spring and summer.

Horned Lark (*Eremophila alpestris*)

Rapid Identification – For males, this small bird has a yellow face, a big black mask, and two tiny hornlike feathers on top of its head. The horns may be raised or lowered. The crown of the head and back of the neck are light brown, and a black band is seen across the chest. The back and wings are tan to brown, and the belly is white. The tail is black with white edges. Females have less color, no horns, and lack the black mask.

Sounds – The song is a musical whistle that gets faster as it's sung and only lasts a few seconds.

Diet – Insects, earthworms, and seeds are eaten.

Season found in Texas – Horned Larks can be found year-round all over Texas. The eastern edge may only see them in the winter.

House Finch (*Haemorhous mexicanus*)

Rapid Identification – The male is a tiny bird with a red head, throat, and chest. The upper belly is red, which blends into brown and white streaks as you move lower. The sides (flanks) are also covered in brown and white streaks. The wings are streaked brown and black. The tail has a small notch and is also brown and black, but is mostly black with white edges.

The female lacks the red and is mostly brown, with brown and white streaks like the male. The female looks very much like the male, except for the red.

Sounds – The males sing a warbled song. It only lasts a few seconds and sounds like a mixture of whistles and peeps. Many little peeps are repeated as a call.

Diet – A wide variety of seeds and fruits are eaten. A few insects are taken.

Season found in Texas – Year round in the western half and near the eastern border.

House Sparrow (*Passer domesticus*)

Rapid Identification – The males have a gray crown, a broad sienna brown patch behind the eyes, a black patch between the eyes and beak (lore), white cheeks, black chin, and throat (bib), gray belly and sides (flanks), brown and black streaked wings, and a tail. The females have a similar pattern but without the brown patch behind the eyes, no black patch between the eyes and beak (lore), and tan instead of brown on the wings and tail.

Sounds – The song is a repeating two syllable "chirp-peep." Most of the singing is done by males. Males and females use the occasional peep sound to communicate with each other.

Diet – Seeds and insects are taken in most areas, but in cities, they will consume food dropped by humans.

Season found in Texas – Year-round in all of Texas.

House Wren (*Troglodytes aedon*)

Rapid Identification – A small, plain, tan to brown, round bodied bird with dark bars on the wings and tail. The beak and tail are short. Males and females look alike.

Sounds – Songs sound like rapid twittering. The call is more of a rapid rattle.

Diet – Insects and spiders are common food items. They have been seen eating snail shells, perhaps for the calcium content.

Season found in Texas – Fall and winter in the southern half of the state and migration through the northern half.

Inca Dove (*Columbina inca*)

Rapid Identification – This is a tiny dove whose feathers are edged in black, giving the bird a scaly appearance. The bird will be gray to a sand color that gives excellent camouflage on the ground. The underside of the wings is chestnut (cinnamon), and the tail is long and thin with white outer tail feathers.

Sounds – The Inca Dove makes a coo that, to some, sounds like they are saying "no hope." When the bird takes to the air, it sounds like the soft rattling of insect wings.

Diet – Inca Doves will only eat seeds. Bird feeders filled with millet, sunflower, and other common seeds will attract them.

Season found in Texas – Year-round resident in all but the Panhandle area.

Indigo Bunting
(*Passerina cyanea*)

Rapid Identification – The male is a small, dark blue bird, which changes to a brighter blue (indigo) further into the breeding season. The wings and tail are dark and largely black. The female is a light brown with darker wings.

Sounds – The male will whistle and warble a short song for a few seconds. Notes are made in pairs and have been described as "what-what, where-where, see it-see it." Calls sound like a rapid "peep."

Diet – Indigo Bunting enjoys insects, spiders, seeds, and berries.

Season found in Texas – Spring and summer in all but the far western areas.

Ladder-backed Woodpecker (*Dryobates scalaris*)

Male   Female

Rapid Identification – The back of this bird has alternating black and white lines that give it a ladder-like appearance. The front of the bird is similar in appearance, but the black is paler, especially closer to the neck. The top of the male's head is red, and the top of the female's head is black.

Sounds – The call is a short "pik."

Male   Female

Diet – Insects, insect larvae, and cactus fruit are eaten.

Season found in Texas – The eastern region of Texas won't see this bird, but the rest of Texas may see it year-round.

Lark Bunting (*Calamospiza melanocorys*)

Rapid Identification – Males are almost entirely black except for a large white stripe down the outer edges of each wing and on the tips of the tail feathers. Nonbreeding males are brown, black, and white with the white wing stripe. Females are brown, black, and white, with a pale to white eyebrow stripe, a dark stripe below each eye, and a white throat. Both have a thick, bluish gray bill.

Sounds – The song is a series of bubbling calls, whistles, and trills. The call is a chattering "weeee."

Diet – Insects, spiders, seeds, and fruits are eaten.

Season found in Texas – The eastern part of Texas won't see this bird; the northern region may see it year-round; and the rest of Texas can see them in the summer.

Lark Sparrow (*Chondestes grammacus*)

Rapid Identification – The center of the head has a white stripe, followed by a chestnut stripe, then a tan stripe above each eye, then a brown patch below each eye, a white stripe on the side of the chin, a black stripe, and a white throat. The chest and belly are white, with a black spot at the top of the sternum. The flanks are tan, and the back is brown with black streaks. The tail is dark, with big white tips at the corners. Juveniles have less color and have streaks on the chest.

Sounds – The song is a mix of whistles, trills, and buzzes. Calls are a soft tink.

Diet – Insects and seeds are eaten.

Season found in Texas – Most of Texas will see this bird year-round. The northern region will see them in the spring and summer.

Lazuli Bunting (*Passerina amoena*)

Rapid Identification – Breeding males have a sky blue head and neck with a black patch between each eye and the bill. The chest and flanks are rust colored and the belly is white. The back is blue, and the wings have a broad white stripe and dark stripes down the wings. The tail is blue with black edges. Nonbreeding males have a rusty color over much of the bird's blue. Females and immature birds are grayish brown above, have a rusty chest and white belly, and may have a little blue on the wings and tail. The forehead is a bit flat, and the bill is cone shaped.

Sounds – The song begins with a series of rapid notes and ends with three or four slower ones.

Diet – Insects, spiders, seeds, and berries are eaten.

Season found in Texas – The western part of Texas may see this bird as it migrates through.

Least Flycatcher (*Empidonax minimus*)

Rapid Identification – This small bird is grayish-olive on top with a white chest and a lemon-yellow belly. The eyes have a thin white eye ring, and the wings have two white wing bars and white stripes. The tail is dark, like the wings, with white edges and a fork in the center.

Sounds – The sound is described as "chebec," and they are known for repeating their call quite often in the warm months.

Diet – Most of the diet is insects, but some berries and seeds are eaten.

Season found in Texas – All of Texas may see this bird as it migrates through.

LeConte's Sparrow
(*Ammospiza leconteii*)

Rapid Identification – The head has a thin white stripe down the center with a dark stripe on either side. The face is yellow to orange in color, with a dark line behind each eye and a dark spot at the end of that line. The throat and chest are yellow, and the belly is white. The back, flanks, and wings are brown with dark streaks. The thin tail is colored like the back.

Sounds – The call consists of two short, high-speed trills that sound like an insect.

Diet – Insects, spiders, and seeds are eaten.

Season found in Texas – The eastern half of Texas may see this bird in the fall and winter.

Lesser Goldfinch (*Spinus psaltria*)

Rapid Identification – For males, the top half of the head is black, and the lower half is dark yellow. The throat, chest, and belly are all bright yellow. The top of the back is dark yellow, and the wings are black with white spots. The underside of the wings flashes a white spot when the bird is in flight. The tail is thick and black. Females are more of an olive yellow with dark wings and white streaks.

Sounds – The song is a rapid twittering of high-pitched whistles. The call is a rapid 'tee-tee-tee."

Diet – Seeds make up most of the diet, but they will also eat berries.

Season found in Texas – Southwest Texas can see this bird year-round.

Lincoln's Sparrow (*Melospiza lincolnii*)

Rapid Identification – The head has a thin white streak down the center with brown stripes on either side. The face is gray with a brown stripe behind each eye, a second one below each cheek, and a thin eye ring. The throat, chest, and flanks are gray to tan with dark streaks. The belly is white and has little to no streaks. The back and wings are brown, with streaks of black and white. The tail is thin and colored like the back.

Sounds – The song is a mixture of whistles and gurgles that rises in the middle and drops at the end. The call is a quick "chip."

Diet – Insects and seeds are eaten.

Season found in Texas – Texas may see this bird in the fall and winter.

Loggerhead Shrike (*Lanius ludovicianus*)

Rapid Identification – The top of the bird is light gray, and the bottom is white. A black mask runs from the beak, through the eyes, and to the back of the head. The body is thick, the head is large, and the stout, black beak is strongly hooked at the tip. The wings are black with large white patches that are easily seen in flight.

Sounds – They will produce different musical notes, trills, rasps, and buzzes. A rapid, two syllable, soft whistle is common.

The lizard above has been impaled on barbed wire by a Loggerhead Shrike.

Diet – Insects, amphibians, reptiles, small mammals, and birds are eaten. This will include lizards, frogs, snakes, turtles, sparrows, small squirrels, mice, and more.

Season found in Texas – Year-round throughout Texas.

Long-billed Thrasher (*Toxostoma longirostre*)

Rapid Identification – The top of the head and neck are rusty brown, as are the back, wings, and tail. The face is gray, the eyes are bright yellow, and the bill is long, slightly curved, and black. The throat, chest, and belly are white with black spots. The wings are rusty brown with two thin wing stripes that are white with black edges. The tail is long, thin, and brown.

Sounds – The song is a warbled bundle of phrases, trills, and squeaks.

Diet – The diet consists of insects, spiders, snails, fruits, berries, and lizards.

Season found in Texas – South Texas can see this bird year-round.

Long-eared Owl (*Asio otus*)

Rapid Identification – This owl is a bit longer and thinner than most owls. The ear tufts are longer and closer together than what is seen on other owls; the facial disc is orange; and the eyes are yellow. The feathers are a mottling of black, brown, white (gray), and orange. The belly, back, and wings have black vertical streaks that mimic the dark spaces between tree bark. The wings and back may show spots. This pattern makes for great camouflage when the bird is perched.

Sounds – The male's call is a single "whoo" with a 2-4 second pause before producing another. The female's call is very different. It's a high pitched call that sounds like a bleating lamb.

Diet – Small mammals like mice, rats, small birds, reptiles, and rabbits are commonly consumed.

Season found in Texas – Texas may see this owl in the fall and winter.

Louisiana Waterthrush (*Parkesia motacilla*)

Rapid Identification – This small warbler is brown above and white below, with brown streaks. There is a white eyebrow streak that is thin in the front and wide in the rear. The body is round, the legs are long, and the tail is short and squared.

Sounds – Males sing a 2-4 note whistle followed by a descending jumble. The call is a fast, metallic chip.

Diet – This bird has a varied diet that will include mayflies, craneflies, butterflies, moths, aphids, dragonflies, spiders, crawfish, earthworms, minnows, frogs, salamanders, and much more.

Season found in Texas – Spring and summer along the eastern edge near Louisiana. Migration along the Gulf of Mexico.

MacGillivray's Warbler
(*Geothlypis tolmiei*)

Rapid Identification – Males have a black head and neck that look like a hood. The eyes have white crescents above and below them, and the throat has a little white and black scattered about. The area between the eyes and the bill is darker than the rest of the face. The chest and belly of the bird are yellow, with darker shades scattered about. The wings and tail are dark yellow with black streaks. Females and immature birds will have a grayish-brown head and neck and less color.

Sounds – The song is a rapid "tree-tree-tree-twee-twee" that falls off at the end. The song only lasts a few seconds.

Diet – Insects and insect larvae are eaten.

Season found in Texas – West Texas may see this bird as it migrates through.

Marsh Wren (*Cistothorus palustris*)

Rapid Identification – This little wren has a tan patch on top of the head with dark streaks on either side. The eyes have a white eyebrow stripe, the face is gray to tan, and the bill is thin and pointed. The throat, chest, and belly are white to gray, and the flanks are brown. The middle of the back is black with white spots, and the brown wings and tail have black wing bars. The tail is often held up, flicked about, or maybe pulled over the head.

Sounds – The song is a gurgle, ending with a mechanical-like chatter. Calls are a quick chip.

Diet – Insects, spiders, and vegetation are eaten.

Season found in Texas – Northeast Texas will see this bird as it migrates through. The rest of Texas will see it in the fall and winter.

Mississippi Kite (*Ictinia mississippiensis*)

Rapid Identification – The head, neck, back, and belly are all light gray on this small raptor. The primary feathers and the tail are dark gray to black. The inner wing feathers (secondary and tertial feathers) are gray like the rest of the body.

Sounds – The call will be a high, two syllable whistle. The first note is short, and the second one drops in pitch.

Diet – Mississippi Kites will eat insects, small reptiles, amphibians, small birds, bats, and small mammals. They will catch insects in the air and eat them without bothering to land.

Season found in Texas – Spring and summer in the Panhandle region, and migration through all but the far west of Texas.

Mountain Bluebird (*Sialia currucoides*)

Male   Female

Rapid Identification – Males are a beautiful sky-blue, with the underside being a light blue and from above a darker blue. The blue on the underside of the males fades to white near the bottom of the belly. From above, the wing tips are black and easily seen when the bird is perched. Females are gray-brown with blue in the wings and tail, but far less than what is seen in males. Females and immature birds may have a rusty throat, chest, and flanks. Juveniles are similar to females but have white spots on their backs.

Sounds – The song is a soft warble. Calls are a rapid "tew-tew."

Diet – Insects, seeds, and fruits are eaten.

Season found in Texas – Northern and western areas of Texas may see this bird in the fall and winter.

Mourning Dove (*Zenaida macroura*)

Rapid Identification – A medium sized yard bird that is a light peach on the head and body. The wings and back are a darker gray, and the wings have large, irregular black spots. From below, the wing tips and the first half of the tail are black, while the tail tips are white. Males and females are very similar. Females have a little less color and aren't as vocal as most males, and the males may be seen courting females.

Sounds – This bird gets its name from the unique, sad, mourning call it makes. The sound is described as a soft cooing and is one of the most widely known bird sounds in the world. The wings make an unmistakable whistling sound when the bird flies overhead.

Diet – Seeds and grains make up almost all of the dove's diet.

Season found in Texas – Year-round throughout Texas.

Nashville Warbler (*Leiothlypis ruficapilla*)

Rapid Identification – Males have a gray head with a small amount of chestnut on the top. The eyes have white eye rings, the bill is gray, the neck is gray, and the throat, chest, and belly are bright yellow. The back is gray with a little yellow, and the wings and back are brown to black with yellow, but no wing bars are present. Females and immature birds are paler than males.

Sounds – The song is "see-bit see-bit see-bit see-bit" followed by a trill-like whistle.

Diet – Insects and some worms are eaten.

Season found in Texas – This bird can be seen across all of Texas as it migrates through.

Northern Cardinal (*Cardinalis cardinalis*)

Rapid Identification – The male is a large bright red bird with a tall red head crest, bright orange beak, and black mask. The wings and tail will have some dark feathers mixed in with the red. The female is tan with less of a dark mask. She will have a little red on top of her crest and some in the wing feathers and tail.

Sounds – The call contains a series of different high pitched sounds. The first two sounds are often a whistle like sound, followed by two faster chirps, and then, lastly, a rapid trill. Something like "srrr-srrr-tear-tear-whir-whir-whir-whir." Some describe it as a "whistle-whistle-cheer-cheer-whir-whir-whir-whir."

Diet – Northern Cardinals have a varied diet that includes seeds, insects, fruits, and more.

Season found in Texas – Year-round throughout the state.

Northern Flicker (Yellow-Shafted) (*Colaptes auratus*)

Rapid Identification – This is a large gray or brown woodpecker with amazing colors. The head is gray and beige, with a patch of red on the back of the head (nape) and a black mark behind the beak (whisker). The belly is light colored and heavily spotted. The wings and tail are a golden yellow when seen from below. From above, the wings are gray or brown with black bars. Females lack the black stripe behind the beak (whisker).

Sounds – The call is a repeating and rapid "wick-a, wick-a." The song is a 7 to 8 second rolling rattle. A "kyeer" or "ki ki ki" song is produced.

Diet – Ants are a favorite food of this bird, which is probably why it's commonly seen on the ground. This woodpecker will break into ant beds to get the larvae deep inside. Beetles are another commonly selected food. Berries and seeds are eaten in winter.

Season found in Texas – Year-round in the eastern half of the state. Fall and winter in the western half.

Northern Mockingbird (*Mimus polyglottos*)

Rapid Identification – A medium sized bird with a gray back and white belly. The head is also gray on top and white below. The wings are dark with two white wing bars. The tail is long, dark above, and white below. Males and females look alike.

Sounds – The most common call of the mockingbird is a rapid "chew" sound. A raspy and harsh "check" sound may be made at intruders. Mockingbirds like to repeat a phrase several times before moving on to the next one. They will sing for long periods of time. Listen for repetitions in their songs.

Diet – Their diet consists mostly of insects, but berries are taken in the winter. Spiders, worms, crawfish, and small lizards may also be eaten.

Season found in Texas – Year-round throughout the state.

Northern Parula (*Setophaga americana*)

Rapid Identification – This little warbler has a blue-gray head with white crescents above and below each eye and a yellow throat. On the front, the chest is yellow with a dark rusty band across it, and the belly is white. The top of the back has a yellow patch, and the lower part of the back is blue-gray. The wings are blue-gray with two white wing bars, and the tail is also blue-gray. Both wings and tail have dark streaks. Females lack the blue-gray color, except for some on the wings.

Sounds – One call is a rising trill that drops at the end. Bzzzzzz-zip. Calls consist of short chips.

Diet – Insects, seeds, berries, and nectar are eaten.

Season found in Texas – East Texas may see this bird in the spring and summer. Central Texas may see them as they migrate through.

Northern Rough-winged Swallow
(*Stelgidopteryx serripennis*)

Rapid Identification – The top of this bird is all brown, with the wings and tail being darker. The throat and chest are white with a light brown tint, and the belly is white. The eyes are black, and the bill is tiny, sharp, and black. The wings are long and pointed. The tail is short and square. Juveniles have a light cinnamon on the wings.

Sounds – The call is a rapid and repeated brrrret-brrrret-brrrrret.

Diet – Flying insects are taken from the air and often over water.

Season found in Texas – Texas will see this bird in the spring and summer. Along the Gulf of Mexico, the bird may be seen year-round.

Northern Waterthrush (*Parkesia noveboracensis*)

Rapid Identification – The head is brown on top with a pale yellow eyebrow stripe beneath it, and a second stripe may be seen running from the bill to the chin. The face and neck are a mottling of brown and pale yellow. The chest and belly may be white or pale yellow with dark brown streaks. The back and tail are brown, and the legs are long.

Sounds – The song sounds like "chee-chee-chee, chip-chip-chip, chew-chew-chew." The call is a repeating chink.

Diet – Insects, insect larvae, spiders, fish, and salamanders.

Season found in Texas – Texas may see this bird as it migrates through.

Olive-sided Flycatcher
(*Contopus cooperi*)

Rapid Identification – The head is gray, with the top of the head being a little darker. The chin is white, and the neck has a white collar. The front of the bird is gray, with a white area down the center. The back is gray, and the wings are dark with white edges. The tail is dark, almost black.

Sounds – The song is made up of three whistles that some describe as saying "quick-three-beers." Calls are two or three pips.

Diet – Insects and berries are eaten.

Season found in Texas – West Texas may see this bird in the spring and summer.

Olive Sparrow (*Arremonops rufivirgatus*)

Rapid Identification – The center of the head has an olive-gray stripe with brown stripes on either side. Above each eye is another olive-gray stripe, a brown stripe through each eye, and gray cheeks and throat. From below, the bird is olive-gray on the chest and belly, with the lower parts of the belly being whiter. The back and wings are olive, with a few dark streaks.

Sounds – The song is a series of chips that get faster towards the end. Calls are a repeated metallic chip.

Diet – Insects, seeds, and spiders are eaten.

Season found in Texas – The far southern parts of Texas may see this bird year-round.

Orange-crowned Warbler (*Leiothlypis celata*)

Rapid Identification – The head is greenish-yellow to olive-yellow with a yellow line through each eye, a yellow throat, and a tiny bill. From above, the bird is greenish-yellow to olive-yellow, with dark streaks on the wings and tail. From below, the bird is yellow with some dark streaks. Young birds are grayer.

Sounds – The song is a trill that goes up and then down. The call is a chip.

Diet – Insects, spiders, seeds, berries, and sap are eaten.

Season found in Texas – Northern parts of Texas will see this bird as it migrates through. All other regions will see it in the fall and winter.

Orchard Oriole (*Icterus spurius*)

Male   Female

Rapid Identification – The male has a black head, neck, upper back, wings, and tail. The chest, belly, and lower part of the back are chestnut colored. The females are yellow to greenish yellow with dark wings and two white wing bars. Females are more yellow on the front and greenish yellow on the back.

Sounds – The song is a rapid warble or whistling. Chucks and chatters are also made.

Male   Female

Diet – Insects, spiders, nectar, and fruits are eaten.

Season found in Texas – Spring and summer throughout the state.

Ovenbird (*Seiurus aurocapilla*)

Rapid Identification – The center of the head has an orange stripe with thin black stripes on both sides. The face is olive-brown, the eyes have a white eye ring, and the throat is white with a black stripe on both sides. The chest, flanks, and top half of the belly are white with bold black spots and streaks. The back is olive-brown, as are the wings and tail, but with dark streaks.

Sounds – The song is described as "tea-tea-tea" or "tea-cher, tea-cher, tea-cher." The call is a chip or a tink.

Diet – Insects and insect larvae are eaten.

Season found in Texas – All but west Texas will see this bird as it migrates through.

Painted Bunting (*Passerina ciris*)

Rapid Identification – The Painted Bunting may be the most colorful bird to be seen in North America. For males, much of the head and neck are blue, with a red throat, chest, belly, and rump. The back, wings, and tail are different shades of green and yellow. Females and immature birds are bright green with a pale ring around each eye.

Sounds – The song is short, lasts about two seconds, and is a series of musical, high pitched notes.

Male   Female

Diet – Seeds are eaten for most of the year, but insects are taken more often in the breeding season. Insects are higher in protein than seeds, so this is common among many bird species. They will forage along the ground for bugs, spiders, flies, beetles, wasps, and more.

Season found in Texas – Spring and summer in all but a few western areas.

Pileated Woodpecker (*Dryocopus pileatus*)

Male   Male

Rapid Identification – A large woodpecker with a black body, a black and white striped head, and a tall red crest (mohawk). The male has a red check stripe, whereas the female lacks this.

Sounds – The drumming sound made as the bird makes holes in trees is often the first sound heard. The call is a rapid and loud "cuk-cuk, cuk-cuk-cuk." The call is sometimes compared to a maddening shriek. Most would agree that the sound is loud and annoying.

Female on left. Male on right.   Female

Diet – The woodpecker is often heard before it's seen because it slams (drums) its beak into wood in search of a meal. Carpenter ants are a favorite food for this bird. Besides ants and beetle larvae, fruits, insects, and nuts will be eaten. The ability of the woodpecker to hammer deep into a tree gives it the ability to reach food items unavailable to other animals.

Season found in Texas – Year-round near the Louisiana border.

Pine Siskin (*Spinus pinus*)

Rapid Identification – A small brown bird with dark streaks over most of the body. The chest and belly are lighter, and the back is darker. The wings and tail have yellow streaks. Males and females look the same.

Sounds – This bird makes a peculiar "bzzzzzzt" call. The call sounds a bit electric.

Diet – Pine seeds are a favorite of this bird, and give it part of its name. They will take the seeds of other trees and grasses when needed. Insects, spiders, grubs, ash, salt, and cement will also be eaten.

Season found in Texas – Fall and winter throughout the state.

Pine Warbler (*Setophaga pinus*)

Rapid Identification – A tiny yellow bird with gray wings. The yellow is brighter on the chest and belly but darker (olive) on the head, back, and sides (flanks). The gray wings have two white wing bars. The female is similar to the male but is less yellow. The bird is large for a warbler.

Sounds – The song is a rapid trill lasting about two seconds. A sharp chip call may also be heard.

Female

Males

Diet – Caterpillars, insects, and spiders are eaten when the months are warm. Seeds (mostly pine) and fruits are taken in the colder months.

Season found in Texas – Year-round near the Louisiana border. Fall and winter along the Gulf of Mexico.

Prairie Falcon (*Falco mexicanus*)

Rapid Identification – The top of the head is light brown, above each eye is a white eyebrow stripe, and the eyes and bill are surrounded by yellow. Above the bill is a white area; the cheeks are white; below each cheek is a brown stripe; and the throat is white. The front of the bird is white with brown vertical streaks. The back, wing, and tail are brown, with white edges on the feathers. When in flight, look for large brown patches in the armpit area.

Sounds – Calls may include a shrill "kri-kri-kri," a shriek, or a "raa-raa-raa" repeated over and over.

Diet – Small mammals, birds, and insects are eaten.

Season found in Texas – Western parts of Texas may see this falcon year-round. Other regions may only see it in the winter.

Prothonotary Warbler (*Protonotaria citrea*)

Rapid Identification – This warbler has a surprising bright golden yellow color and gray to black (blue-gray) wings with thin white edges. The undertail coverts are white, and the body is a little thick. The bill is dark to black and a little thicker than what is seen in most warblers. Females are a little less yellow and more black, making them not as bright as the males.

Sounds – The song is a loud, high-pitched "tweet" repeated four times.

Diet – The diet consists of spiders, flies, moths, butterflies, beetles, grasshoppers, ants, snails, mollusks, and some fruits.

Season found in Texas – Spring and summer in the eastern half of the state. Fall and winter near the Gulf of Mexico.

Purple Martin (*Progne subis*)

Rapid Identification – An iridescent, dark blue or purple bird with black wings and long black tail. The chest and belly are black on the male. The females have less color than the males and aren't as dark. The chest and belly of the females are white with dark vertical streaks.

Sounds – The Purple Martin is known for being noisy. Half of its time in the air seems to be filled with noisy chatter. The song is described as a "liquid gurgling warble."

Diet – Flying insects. Dragonflies seem to be a large part of the diet.

Season found in Texas – Spring and summer over all but the western edges of Texas.

Pyrrhuloxia (*Cardinalis sinuatus*)

Rapid Identification – This cardinal relative looks half cardinal and half parrot. The top of the head has a tall red crest, and the top half of the head, rear of the head, and cheeks are gray. The eyes and the area in front of them are covered by a red mask, and the bill is bright yellow. The throat, chest, and belly are bright red. The flanks and back are gray, and the wings are mostly gray except for a red patch. Much more red is seen in the wings during flight. The tail is long, dark, and red. Females lack the red mask, and most of the red in other places.

Sounds – The song is very similar to the northern cardinal "teer-teer-teer-teer," but shorter. Calls are a quick pip.

Diet – Insects, seeds, fruit, nectar, and pollen are eaten.

Season found in Texas – Western and southern Texas can see this bird year-round.

Red-bellied Woodpecker (*Melanerpes carolinus*)

Rapid Identification – A medium sized woodpecker with a broad red stripe on top of the head (crown) and down the back of the neck (nape). The face, chest, and belly are white. The back, wings, and tail are barred in black and white. Females don't have red on top of the head but do have it down the back of the head and neck.

Sounds – The call is a rapid "kwirrrr" sound. Other sounds can be a "ka" sound with a second or two between the calls. Rapid, short drums will also be heard.

Female

Male left and female right.

Diet – Insects, spiders, nuts, pinecones, fruits, and berries. Occasionally, they will take lizards, birds, and minnows.

Season found in Texas – Year-round in the eastern 1/3 of Texas.

Red-breasted Nuthatch (*Sitta canadensis*)

Rapid Identification – A small, round bird with black and white head stripes, a rust colored breast (similar to the color of a robin), a blue-gray back and wings, and a very short tail. The female is lighter in all of the colors, so she is more gray than blue and more tan than rust.

Sounds – The call is described as a nasally "yank-yank" sound coming out of a tin horn. Usually, 4 to 6 yanks will be made before there is a pause.

Diet – Insects and spiders in the summer and conifer seeds in the winter.

Season found in Texas – Fall and winter in most of Texas. They are absent from the southern 1/3 of the state.

Red Crossbill (*Loxia curvirostra*)

Male   Female

Rapid Identification – This odd-looking finch has a bill that crosses over, making it look odd and twisted. Males are red with dark wings and a short, dark tail. It is gray around the cheeks, in front of the eyes, and behind the eyes. Some individuals will have two white wing bars. Females have the red replaced with yellow. Young birds are dark gray and have a white belly with dark vertical streaks. Males nearing maturity will be more of a red-orange color.

Sounds – The songs are a mixture of warbles and trills. Calls are a repeating chip.

Diet – The odd bill of this bird is specialized for tearing into pinecones. The seeds of many cone-bearing trees are eaten.

Season found in Texas – North and west Texas may see this bird in the winter.

Red-eyed Vireo (*Vireo olivaceus*)

Rapid Identification – The top of the head is a large gray patch edged with black, and above each eye is a large white eyebrow stripe. The bright red eyes have a dark stripe running through them, and the cheeks are olive-green to gray. The throat, chest, and belly are white. The back, wings, and tail are olive-green, and the wings have dark streaks.

Sounds – The song is a series of whistles that sound as if the bird is calling to someone or asking a question. The call is a loud buzz.

Diet – Insects, spiders, snails, seeds, and fruits are eaten.

Season found in Texas – East Texas will see this bird in spring and summer. All but west Texas will see them as they migrate through.

161

Red-headed Woodpecker (*Melanerpes erythrocephalus*)

Rapid Identification – A medium sized woodpecker with a red head and neck, a black back, black and white wings, a white chest and belly, and a black tail. Males and females look alike.

Sounds – A loud and repeated "chur-chur" or "yarrow-yarrow" followed by drumming is often heard. The call is shriller than the Red-bellied Woodpecker.

Diet – Insects, fruits, seeds, acorns, fruits, mice, birds, and more.

Season found in Texas – Year-round in the panhandle and eastern part of the state. Fall and winter in the central region of Texas.

Red-shouldered Hawk (*Buteo lineatus*)

Rapid Identification – A medium sized hawk with reddish brown feathers covering the head, neck, chest, belly, and wing lining. When flying, the wings and tail are heavily barred in black and white when seen from below. The borders of the wings and tail have a broad black band. When perched, the wings are mostly reddish brown with an irregular scattering of black and white patches. Females are 25% to 30% larger than males.

Sounds – A shrill scream or a "kee-yaar" call is often heard.

Diet – Amphibians, reptiles, birds, and small mammals will be taken. Fish and large insects are taken less often.

Season found in Texas – Year-round in the eastern half of Texas.

Red-tailed Hawk (*Buteo jamaicensis*)

Rapid Identification – A large hawk, brown above and white below, with a large reddish (rusty) tail. The wing tips are black with white edges, and below the chest is an irregular dark bar.

Sounds – A high pitched scream that sounds like "keeeeer." If you have ever heard a hawk call, you have probably heard this one.

Diet – Small mammals, birds, and reptiles, especially snakes. Small prey will be taken to an elevated position to be eaten. Bats and frogs are occasionally taken. Rodents and snakes make up a large part of the diet.

Season found in Texas – Year-round throughout the state.

Red-winged Blackbird (*Agelaius phoeniceus*)

Rapid Identification – The male is a small black bird with bright red-orange shoulder patches bordered in yellow to the rear. The females are brown birds with brown and white streaks all over the chest and belly. The face is a light tan to yellow with a tan eyebrow stripe, and the shoulder has a tiny red patch. This patch is nowhere near the size of what is seen on the male and may be difficult to see at all. The female has a wing bar made up of black squares bordered in white. The female looks more like a sparrow than this bird.

Sounds – The male is often seen as it lets out a rapid, shrill "conk-la-ree" call. Spend some time on a bayou, swamp, or similar habitat, and you will hear the call of the Red-Winged Blackbird. Rapid, high pitched "peeps" or "chucks" can be heard when the bird is frightened.

Female and male

Diet – Insects, grains, seeds, spiders, snails, worms, crawfish, frogs, lizards, fruit, and berries will be consumed.

Season found in Texas – Year-round throughout the state.

Rock Wren (*Salpinctes obsoletus*)

Rapid Identification – The top of the head is brown with a light eyebrow stripe beneath it. A dark stripe runs through each eye, and below that, the face is white to tan. The throat and chest are white with tiny dark spots or dark streaks. The back, wings, and tail are brown with speckled black and white spots. Thin black bars are found on the wings and tail.

Sounds – The song is a mixture of "tree-tree-tree-tree, turs, and trills." The call is a repeating "trrrr."

Diet – Insects, spiders, seeds, and plants are eaten.

Season found in Texas – West and central Texas may see this bird year-round.

Rose-breasted Grosbeak (*Pheucticus ludovicianus*)

Male Female

Rapid Identification – Males have a black head, neck, back, wings, and tail, with some white in the wings. The throat and sternum are bright red, while the belly, undertail coverts, and underside of the tail are white. Females are dark brown on top, pale, and streaked below, with a white eyebrow streak. Both birds have thick, heavy, pale beaks.

Sounds – The song lasts 6-20 seconds and consists of rapid whistles that rise and fall. Calls often sound like a rapid squeak.

Male and female

Diet – Insects are preferred, but seeds and fruit are also eaten. The diet includes butterflies, moths, bees, ants, berries, and many seed types.

Season found in Texas – This is a migratory bird in all but the western edge of Texas.

Rough-legged Hawk (*Buteo lagopus*)

Rapid Identification – A large hawk that is mottled brown (reddish brown) and white above and mostly white below. The wing lining is dark, while the rest of the wings are white. The trailing edge of all feathers is black, and the tail is mostly white with a dark band at the tip. Look for two black patches at the base of the primary feathers (wrist). The wrist patches and white tail with a dark band on the edge are good identifying characteristics.

Sounds – The call is a loud catlike "meow."

Diet – Their diet will consist of lemmings, squirrels, rabbits, and similar animals.

Season found in Texas – This bird may be seen in the fall and winter in all but the far southern parts of Texas.

Ruby-crowned Kinglet (*Corthylio calendula*)

Rapid Identification – A tiny olive-green bird with black and yellow on the wings, white and black wing bars, and a bright red thin crown stripe (mohawk when raised). The red crown stripe is only on the male. A white eye ring and white wing bars are good identifying marks. Often, the female is not as dark as the male and is more yellow. Also, the female doesn't have the red crown stripe.

Sounds – The Ruby-crowned Kinglet sings a repetitive chirping song of 2 or 3 notes. Each note gets higher and louder, and the song lasts a total of about five seconds.

Diet – Insects, wasps, ants, spiders, seeds, and fruits are eaten.

Season found in Texas – Fall and winter throughout the state.

Ruby-throated Hummingbird (*Archilochus colubris*)

Male   Female

Rapid Identification – A very tiny and very fast bird with a green head, red throat, white chest, green back, green belly, and black tipped tail. Females lack the bright red throat and have less color than males.

Sounds – Hummingbirds are difficult to hear unless they are close. A series of very rapid, high pitched chirps are made. They are most often heard when two males come into contact with each other. At that time, you can hear them complaining with angry chirps. You may also hear the humming of the wings.

Female and male

Diet – Nectar from flowers and small insects.

Season found in Texas – Spring and summer in the eastern half of Texas and migratory in the central region.

Rufous-crowned Sparrow (*Aimophila ruficeps*)

Rapid Identification – The top of the head is rusty brown, and below it is a white eyebrow stripe. The eyes have a white eye ring; a dark stripe runs behind each eye; the face is gray; and the chin has a white stripe with a black stripe below it. The chest and belly are grayish-brown. The back is brown with gray edges. The wings and tail are brown with some dark stripes.

Sounds – The song is a mixture of squeaks, chirps, and chatters. The call is a repetitive "trrr."

Diet – Insects, seeds, and plants are eaten.

Season found in Texas – This sparrow may be seen in parts of north, central, and west Texas.

171

Rufous Hummingbird (*Selasphorus rufus*)

Rapid Identification – The top of the male's head is dark, the face is rusty-orange, a small white spot is behind each eye, the bill is thin, straight, and needle-like, and the throat is red to orange. The chest and area under the tail are white, and the belly is rusty-orange. The back is rusty-orange, the wings are dark, and the tail comes to a point when perched. The tips of the tail feathers are black and sometimes end in white spots. The top half of the female's head is green, and the lower half is white with green spots. The flanks have a rusty tint, the back is green with some rusty patches, and the wings are black.

Sounds – The call is a rapid "chu-chu-chu" or "chee."

Diet – Nectar and insects are eaten.

Season found in Texas – This bird may be seen migrating through the far western parts of Texas.

172

Rusty Blackbird (*Euphagus carolinus*)

Rapid Identification – Breeding males are all black and may look a little green in the right light. The eyes are yellow and bright. Nonbreeding males are dark brown with dark spots all over. The bill, legs, wings, and tail are black, and a pale eyebrow stripe is often seen. Some males have less color on the head and body. Females are tan close to the head and darker near the tail. The area around her eyes is dark, and a pale eyebrow stripe is seen. Her wings and tail are dark.

Sounds – The song is a squeaky, metallic series of notes. The call is a "chek."

Diet – Insects, seeds, and fruit are eaten.

Season found in Texas – East Texas may see this bird in the fall and winter.

Sage Thrasher (*Oreoscoptes montanus*)

Rapid Identification – The top of the head is gray, the eyes are yellow, a faint white line runs through each eye, the cheeks are brown, and the chin is white. The throat, chest, and belly are white and covered in small black spots that form vertical streaks. The flanks are a little rusty, and the back is grayish brown. The wings are brown with white edges on the feathers and have two thin white wing bars. The tail is thin and brown.

Sounds – The song is a long, complex mixture of notes and phrases. The call is a quick "chuck."

Diet – Insects and berries are eaten.

Season found in Texas – All but the northern and eastern most parts of Texas may see this bird in the fall and winter.

174

Savannah Sparrow
Passerculus sandwichensis

Rapid Identification – This sparrow has a brown cap, a yellow streak above each eye, brown cheeks bordered in black, and a white throat. The chest is white with brown vertical streaks and a brown spot in the center of the chest. The belly below is white. The back and tail are brown with dark streaks.

Sounds – The song is described as a "tsip-tsip-tsip-seeerrr." Calls are short chips.

Diet – Insects, spiders, and seeds are eaten.

Season found in Texas – All of Texas may see this bird in the fall and winter.

Say's Phoebe (*Sayornis saya*)

Rapid Identification – From above, this bird is brownish gray, with the head being darker than the body. The wings are darker than the body, and the wing feathers have white edges. The tail is gray in flight, black when perched, and has a small fork. From below, the chest is gray with a little cinnamon mixed in. The belly is cinnamon and brighter under the tail.

Sounds – The song is a simple two-syllable whistle. The call is a slurred whistle.

Diet – These birds enjoy a diet of insects. The insects may be taken in the air or from the ground.

Season found in Texas – Western and southern areas of Texas may see this bird in the fall and winter. Far west Texas can see them year-round.

Scarlet Tanager (*Piranga olivacea*)

Male   Female

Rapid Identification – Breeding males have an unmistakable two color combination of scarlet red and black. The head, neck, and body are all scarlet red, while their eyes, wings, and tail are all black. Females are olive yellow except for the dark wings and tail.

Sounds – The song is a series of rapid warbles that are compared to the song of a robin. The sound is a bit nasally and like a chirp.

Female   Male

Diet – Insects make up most of the diet, but some fruit and young buds are also eaten. The diet includes butterflies, moths, beetles, flies, termites, dragonflies, snails, earthworms, and spiders.

Season found in Texas – Migratory through the eastern half of the state.

Scissor-tailed Flycatcher (*Tyrannus forficatus*)

Rapid Identification – A long, slender bird with a white to pale gray head and neck, a white to pale gray chest and upper belly, salmon pink flanks and lower belly, dark wings, and the most amazing, extremely long, deeply forked, black and white scissor tail you have ever seen. Females have a shorter tail (30%) and are a little whiter. Juveniles have short tails.

Sounds – The song is an irregular series of rapid notes that sound like someone is pinching a squeaky toy. The song starts slow, speeds up, and only lasts a few seconds. Chirps and chirrs will also be made.

Diet – Mostly insects and some berries.

Season found in Texas – Spring and summer throughout the state.

Scott's Oriole (*Icterus parisorum*)

Rapid Identification – Males have a black head, neck, and chest. The area around the shoulders, flanks, and belly is bright yellow. The back is black, and the feathers there have white edges. The wings are black, with vertical white streaks and two white wingbars. From below, the tail is bright yellow, and from above, it is black. Females lack the black head, neck, and chest and have a duller yellow color.

Sounds – The song is a short, flute-like series of notes that only last a few seconds. The call is a short "chick."

Diet – Insects, fruit, and nectar are all eaten.

Season found in Texas – Central and west Texas can see this bird in the spring and summer.

Sharp-shinned Hawk (*Accipiter striatus*)

Rapid Identification – This is a small hawk with short wings and a very long tail. The top of the head, back, and wings are a dark blue gray. The neck, chest, and belly are covered in horizontal rusty bars. Look for the very long tail with four broad black bands. This bird is a little bigger than a robin.

Sounds – Males and females will produce a series of "kik-kik-kik" whistling calls. The male has a slightly higher sound to his voice than the female.

Diet – Songbirds make up 90% of the diet. Any bird up to the size of a robin may be taken. They will also eat rodents and insects.

Season found in Texas – They may be seen across Texas in the fall and winter.

Short-eared Owl (*Asio flammeus*)

Rapid Identification – This is a medium sized owl with tiny ear tufts that often can't be seen. This bird is mottled brown, white, and light orange. The chest and belly are streaked in brown and light orange. The yellow eyes are surrounded by black eye patches. From above, the wings are mottled like the body, and below, they are more white with dark wrist patches and dark wing tips.

Sounds – The primary call is a series of a dozen or so hoots. Another call sounds a little like a kitten meowing. A rough screech will be made when they are irritated.

Diet – Small mammals like mice, rats, and rabbits make up most of the diet. They will also take bats and birds.

Season found in Texas – The Short-eared Owl may be seen in Texas during the fall and winter.

Song Sparrow (*Melospiza melodia*)

Rapid Identification – A small bird, but medium sized for a sparrow. This bird is almost all brown and white, with brown streaks. The head has multiple brown streaks with a tan to white color in between each. The chest and belly are streaked with brown, but the belly is whiter. The wings are brown, with brown streaks and a few black spots. The tail is darker brown than most of the body. Males and females are very similar, but the female tends to be less colorful and more drab.

Sounds – The song is loud for such a small bird. There will first be a few notes, with short pauses between each. After a couple of clanging notes, a rapid trill will follow. Loud, squeaky chips are made when they are annoyed.

Diet – Insects, seeds, and berries.

Season found in Texas – Fall and winter throughout the state.

Spotted Towhee (*Pipilo maculatus*)

Rapid Identification – The head, neck, and throat are black; the eyes are red; and the bill is short and black. The chest is black, the belly is white down the center, and the flanks are a rusty red. The back is black, and the wings are black with white spots. These white spots sometimes form one or two white wing bars. The tail is black above and black below, with white spots on the lateral feathers. Females may be more brown on the head than black, like males.

Sounds – The song is a quick series of three notes, followed by a trill. Some say the song sounds like "drink-your-tee." The call is a cat-like screech.

Diet – Insects, spiders, seeds, and berries are eaten.

Season found in Texas – All but the eastern most parts of Texas may see this bird in the fall and winter.

Summer Tanager (*Piranga rubra*)

Rapid Identification – The male is a bright strawberry red bird with a thick, heavy beak. The head, neck, chest, and belly are all bright red with no distinct markings. The wings are red but darker, and with dark tips on the feathers. The tail looks the same. The female looks the same as the male, except the red of the male is swapped for mustard yellow or perhaps an olive to yellow color.

Sounds – The male will sing a varied whistle lasting several seconds. The song is similar to the American Robin. When agitated, they make a call sounding like "pit-ti-tuck."

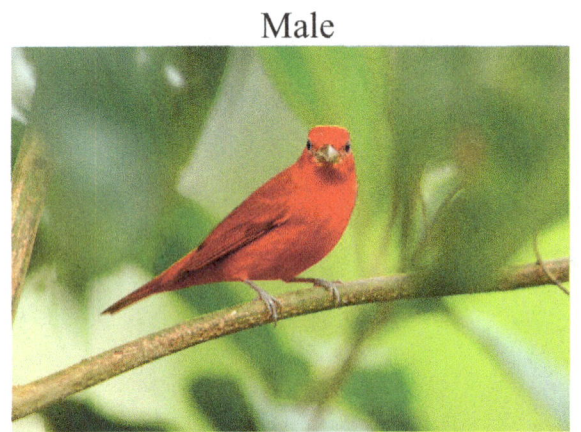

Male   Female

Diet – These birds have a diet that consists mainly of bees and wasps. Other insects, berries, and fruits may also be taken.

Season found in Texas– Spring and summer in all but the panhandle and regions near it.

Swallow-tailed Kite (*Elanoides forficatus*)

Rapid Identification – This elegant bird of prey has a long and slender look to it, along with an incredible, deeply forked tail. The head, neck, chest, and belly are all white and contrast with the rest of the bird, which is all black. From above, the wings are black, and the leading edge of the secondary feathers is darker than the rest. From below, the wing lining is all white, but the rest of the feathers are black. There is a white area at the base of the deeply forked tail (undertail coverts), and the rest of the tail is black.

Sounds – The call is a loud, repeating, squeaky whistle.

Diet – Flying insects make up most of the diet. They will also eat amphibians, reptiles, small birds, bats, fish, and fruit. They will often eat their food while flying.

Season found in Texas – Rarely seen in the southeastern part of the state, near Louisiana.

Swamp Sparrow (*Melospiza georgiana*)

Rapid Identification – The top of the head has a rusty red patch. Above each eye is a patch of gray, and a black line runs behind each eye. Below each eye is a tan to brown patch and a white throat. A gray collar may be seen around the neck. The chest and belly are gray and may have dark vertical streaks. The flanks are rusty red. The back and wings are reddish brown with black vertical streaks. The tail is reddish brown above and below.

Sounds – The song is a rapid series of tweets that sound like a slow trill.

Diet – Insects, seeds, and fruits are eaten.

Season found in Texas – All of Texas may see this bird in the fall and winter.

Townsend's Warbler (*Setophaga townsendi*)

Rapid Identification – The top of the head and throat are black, and the cheeks have a large black patch that is surrounded by yellow and often has a yellow spot inside of it beneath the eye. The chest is yellow with black streaks, and the belly is white with black streaks. The back is a dark yellow, and the wings are black with two white wingbars. From above, the tail is black with white edges, and from below, the tail is white with dark edges. Females have a yellow throat and are not as dark as males.

Sounds – The song first has a "tweee-tweee" repeated three times, followed by two buzzy trills.

Diet – Insects, insect larvae, spiders, nectar, and seeds are eaten.

Season found in Texas – West Texas may see this warbler as it migrates through.

187

Tree Swallow (*Tachycineta bicolor*)

Rapid Identification – The head is metallic blue-green from the top of the head to just beneath the eyes. The eyes are black and have a black spot in front of them. The bill is very small and black. All of the area below the eyes, throat, chest, and belly are snow white. The back and upper region of the wings are metallic blue-green, and the lower region is black. The wings may look black when the bird is in flight. Also, when in flight, two white patches are seen on each side, just before the tail. Females and immature males have far less bright color.

Sounds – The songs are a combination of two liquid chirps and a gurgle. Calls are a rapid, repeating chirp.

Diet – Insects, spiders, some worms, and calcium-containing items like eggshells, exoskeletons, and small bones.

Season found in Texas – Most of Texas can see this bird as it migrates through. The Gulf Coast region may see them in the fall and winter.

Tufted Titmouse (*Baeolophus bicolor*)

Rapid Identification - A small bird that is blue gray on top, white on bottom with rust colored flanks, and a tall blue gray crest on their heads. Males and females look alike.

Sounds – The song is described as sounding like "peter-peter-peter." A metallic sounding whistle is often repeated two or three times before pausing and repeating. A "tee-tee-tee-buzz" call is often made.

Diet – Insects, caterpillars, spiders, snails, seeds, and berries.

Season found in Texas – The eastern half of Texas can see this bird year-round.

Varied Bunting (*Passerina versicolor*)

Rapid Identification – Males have a bluish-purple head with a red crest and a red throat. The area around the bill is black, and the pale bill is thick. The red is scattered about the body, and more is found over the chest and back. The wings and tail are darker than the body and may appear black. Females are tan with darker wings and have none of the color seen in males.

Sounds – The song is a mixture of rising and falling pleasant notes. The call is a quick "peep."

Diet – Insects, seeds, and fruit are eaten.

Season found in Texas – South and west Texas may see this bird in the spring and summer.

Verdin (*Auriparus flaviceps*)

Rapid Identification – Most of this bird's head is yellow except for the rear, which is gray. All of the bird's body is gray, and the wings are dark, with a chestnut red spot at the shoulders. The tail is also dark, like the wings. Juveniles lack the bright colors.

Sounds – The song is composed of three quick notes: "tsee-tsee-tsee." The call is a quick, two-syllable tweet.

Diet – Insects, spiders, fruit, nectar, and plants are all eaten.

Season found in Texas – All but the northern and eastern regions of Texas may see this bird year-round.

Vermilion Flycatcher (*Pyrocephalus rubinus*)

Rapid Identification – Males are a fiery red on top of the head, below the eyes, and on the chin, chest, and belly. The eyes have a dark stripe through them, and the bill is short and thick. The back, wings, and tail are all brown, and the wings have two white wingbars. Females are brown above, white on the front, and have a little red on the belly. Immature females have yellow on the belly.

Sounds – The song is a short one second twitter, and the call is a soft peep.

Male   Female

Diet – Insects are eaten by this bird.

Season found in Texas – Western and southern Texas may see this bird year-round or at different parts of the year.

Vesper Sparrow (*Pooecetes gramineus*)

Rapid Identification – On top, this sparrow is mottled brown, white, and black. The face has a thin, white eyering, and the chin has a thin, white stripe beneath it. The chest is white with brown vertical streaks, and the belly is white. Small rusty patches may be visible at the shoulders. From above, the tail is brown with dark streaks, and from below, it's white. White outer tail feathers are seen when the bird is in flight.

Sounds – The song consists of a few whistles and a falling trill. Calls are chirps.

Diet – Seeds, insects, and spiders are eaten.

Season found in Texas –Texas will see this bird in the fall and winter.

Violet-green Swallow (*Tachycineta thalassina*)

Rapid Identification – For males, the top of the head and back are metallic green, and the rump is purple. The cheeks, throat, chest, and belly are all white. The wings are long and extend far back past the tail when the bird is perched. The tail is dark, has two white patches at the base (from above), and is squared off when the bird is in flight. Females have a brown head, dirty brown cheeks, and not as much color as the males.

Sounds – The song is a squeaky warble, and the call is "chee-chee."

Diet – This bird takes insects from the air to eat.

Season found in Texas – West Texas may see this bird in the spring and summer.

Warbling Vireo (*Vireo gilvus*)

Rapid Identification – The top of the head and back are olive-green, the eyes have a dark eyeline running through each, and the area above and below the eyes is light. The throat, chest, and belly are pale yellow. From above, the wings and tail are olive-green with dark streaks. From below, the tail is yellow. The legs are an odd blue.

Sounds – The song is a variable warbling that lasts about three seconds. The call is a raspy scold.

Diet – Insects, spiders, and berries are eaten.

Season found in Texas – The northern half of Texas can see this bird in spring and summer. The southern half will see them as they migrate through.

Western Kingbird (*Tyrannus verticalis*)

Rapid Identification – The head, neck, throat, and chest are all gray. The small black eyes have a dark line running through them, and the bill is black. The belly is lemon yellow, and the area under the tail is gray. The back is a mix of olive and yellow. The wings are dark with white edges, and the tail is black with white edges.

Sounds – The song is a series of "kips" that begin soft but get louder towards the end. Calls are a squeaky chatter.

Diet – Insects, spiders, and berries are eaten.

Season found in Texas – All but the eastern parts of Texas can see this bird in the spring and summer.

Western Meadowlark (*Sturnella neglecta*)

Rapid Identification – The forehead is very low and isn't much higher than the bill. The top of the head is brown, with a pale stripe above each eye. The eyes have a brown stripe running through them to the back of the head. Breeding adults have a yellow patch in front of the eyes, a yellow throat, a large black V on the chest, and a yellow belly. Nonbreeding and young birds have far less yellow and a faint V. The back, legs, and wings are brown with dark streaks. The short tail has white lateral feathers that are seen in flight.

Sounds – The song starts with three flute like whistles, followed by a gurgle. The call is a "chup."

Diet – Insects, seeds, bird eggs, and roadkill.

Season found in Texas – North and west Texas can see this bird year-round. Other parts may see it in the fall and winter.

Western Screech-Owl (*Megascops kennicottii*)

Rapid Identification – This owl is covered in gray to brown feathers with black streaks. The belly is paler than the back, and black vertical streaks are easily seen. The head is a bit square, the ear tufts are small, the face has black borders, and the eyes are bright yellow.

Sounds – The song is a series of hoots that get faster towards the end. It's often compared to the sound of a ping pong ball dropping and coming to rest. The call is a high pitched chirp.

Diet – Birds, fish, amphibians, reptiles, small mammals, crawfish, and insects are eaten.

Season found in Texas – Central and Western Texas can see this bird year-round.

198

Western Tanager (*Piranga ludoviciana*)

Rapid Identification – Breeding males have a head that is flaming red and blends into yellow as you approach the neck. The neck, chest, and belly are all bright yellow. The wings are black, with a yellow shoulder patch and two white wingbars. The upper half of the back is black, and the lower half is yellow. The tail is black with white streaks. Nonbreeding males lack a red head. Females are yellow with black wings and two white wingbars. Some females are gray-brown with yellow under the tail.

Sounds – The song consists of five or six quick phrases. The call is "pit-r-ick."

Diet – Insects and fruits are eaten.

Season found in Texas – All but east Texas can see this bird as it migrates through.

199

Western Wood-Pewee (*Contopus sordidulus*)

Rapid Identification – This flycatcher is gray all over with a few marks. The head is darker than the body, and the top of the head has a bit of a crest. The chin, center of the belly, and undertail area are white, but the rest of the bird is gray. The long wings are dark and have two white wingbars. The tail is also dark, thin, and has a small fork at the tip.

Sounds – The song is a short, nasally whistle. Some say it sounds like "pee-er."

Diet – This bird eats insects caught in the air.

Season found in Texas – Northern and western Texas can see this bird in the spring and summer.

White-breasted Nuthatch (*Sitta carolinensis*)

Female-blue head stripe Male-black head stripe

Rapid Identification – A small bird with a broad black stripe over the top of the head (crown), which goes down and around the back of the neck. The back, wings, and tail are blue gray, with the wings and tail tipped in black. The face, throat, chest, and belly are white, and there is a rust colored spot on the rear part of the flanks. The females have a blue gray head stripe instead of a black one.

Sounds – The song is a "wha-wha-wha-wha-wha-wha-wha." 6 to 12 notes sounding the same are sung each time. It also produces a loud, rapid, nasally "kank" sound.

Diet – Insects, spiders, and seeds.

Season found in Texas – Year-round in the eastern ¼ of the state. Fall and winter in the Panhandle region.

201

White-crowned Sparrow (*Zonotrichia leucophrys*)

Rapid Identification - A large sparrow with black and white stripes on the head, a gray face, neck, chest, and belly. The wings and tail are brown with dark stripes and white tips. The flanks are tan. The beak is orange to yellow and stands out a bit. Females are a little smaller than males and aren't as bright.

Sounds – This bird can produce many different whistling and buzzing songs. A rapid peep is made when the bird is startled.

Diet – Seeds, grains, fruits, caterpillars, and other insects are eaten.

Season found in Texas – Fall and winter throughout the state.

White-eyed Vireo (*Vireo griseus*)

Rapid Identification – A small songbird with a gray head and bright yellow spots around and in front of the eyes. The back is a mix of yellow and gray, and the belly is a mix of white and yellow. The flanks are more yellow than the belly. The wings are dark, with some yellow, and a black wing bar bordered by two white wing bars is seen. Males and females look the same.

Sounds – The song is a combination of whistles with chips at the beginning and end. Some suggest they sing "Pik-chicka-weew." An angry sounding "zip-zip-zip" may be heard when they are irritated. Some hear the bird saying, "Give me a rain check."

Diet – Insects, caterpillars, spiders, fruits, and berries.

Season found in Texas – Year-round near the Gulf of Mexico. Spring and summer in the eastern 2/3 of Texas.

White-tailed Kite (*Elanus leucurus*)

Rapid Identification – The head is white, and the eyes are set back in the head with a black border on the surrounding feathers. The bill is yellow close to the face, black further out, and strongly hooked. The mouth is bordered in yellow and is often clearly seen up close. From below, the chest, belly, and tail are all white. The wings are white on the secondary feathers close to the body, but the outer primary feathers are dark and have a distinctive black spot at the wrist areas. From above, the back and wings are mostly gray, but the shoulders have large black spots. From above, the tail is gray near the center and white on the outer feathers. Juveniles have a rusty color on the top of their heads and chests.

Sounds – The call is a repeating whistle that sounds like a chirp.

Diet – Small mammals, birds, reptiles, and some insects are eaten.

Season found in Texas – Southern Texas and areas near the Gulf of Mexico can see this bird year-round.

White-throated Sparrow (*Zonotrichia albicollis*)

Rapid Identification - A small bird with a black and white head stripe, a yellow spot in front of each eye, gray cheeks, and a white throat patch. The top of the bird is mostly brown with dark stripes. The belly is brown to gray.
Males have a brighter yellow spot on the face and darker stripes than females.

Sounds – The song is a series of whistles, with the first one being longer than the ones that follow. Some describe their song as sounding like "Oh-sweet-Canada-Canada." A quick peep is given as a call.

Diet – Seeds, insects, spiders, snails, and fruits.

Season found in Texas – Fall and winter throughout the state.

White-tipped Dove (*Leptotila verreauxi*)

Rapid Identification – This dove is similar to others but without some of the distinctive marks that others have. The head, neck, and body are pale gray, with some pink on the head and neck. The eyes are yellow with a blue eye ring and a blue line between each eye and bill. The bill may also appear blue and sometimes black. The wings and tail are darker than the body and appear brown. The wings have white tips but can only be seen when the bird is in flight. The legs are pink, like we see in other doves.

Sounds – The coo of this dove is slower, deeper, and longer than that of other doves.

Diet – Seeds, insects, and fruit are eaten by this dove.

Season found in Texas – Only the southern most parts of Texas can see this dove, but if they do, they can see it year-round.

White-winged Dove (*Zenaida asiatica*)

Rapid Identification – This dove is light brown on the bottom and a little darker on the top. The wings have a long white stripe on the outer edge, the belly is plain and unspotted, and there is a black dash on each cheek below the eyes. The white wing stripe becomes a white patch in flight. The red eyes have a blue eye ring around them. The legs and feet are pink. The lack of wing spots and the white stripe on the wings are easy ways to tell this bird from the Mourning Dove.

Sounds – The song is a sequence of nine or so slurred coos, lasting 5 to 6 seconds.

Diet – Seeds, grains, and berries make up the diet.

Season found in Texas – Spring and summer in the western and central part of Texas.

Willow Flycatcher (*Empidonax traillii*)

Rapid Identification – This small flycatcher is a brownish olive on its head and back. The neck and chest are white, while the belly is white with a little yellow. The wings are dark with two white wingbars, and the tail is dark and slender. The eyes may have a very thin white ring.

Sounds – This bird's song is a good way to identify it. Listen for the distinct "fitz-bew." The call is "pip."

Diet – This bird eats insects and berries.

Season found in Texas – North, west, and central Texas can see this bird in the spring and summer. Other areas may see them as they migrate through.

Wilson's Warbler (*Cardellina pussilla*)

Rapid Identification – Males have a distinctive round black cap on top of their bright yellow heads. The eyes are black, and the bill is very short. The head and neck are bright yellow with a slight wash of gray. The back and belly are yellow but duller than the head. The back may be a little duller than the belly area. The wings are dark yellow with black streaks, and so is the tail. Females and young birds lack the black cap seen in males. Some females may have a black cap, but the cap is smaller than the one on males.

Sounds – The song is a quick series of 7-8 "chips."

Diet – Insects, spiders, and liquids secreted by scale insects are eaten.

Season found in Texas – This bird can be seen across all of Texas as it migrates through.

209

Winter Wren (*Troglodytes hiemalis*)

Rapid Identification – This small, round bird has a brown cap, a white eyebrow stripe, a dark line behind each eye, and pale cheeks with brown spots. The chin is white, but the chest and belly are brown with black and white marks. The top of the bird is a darker brown than what is seen below, and black bars are found on the wings and stubby tail.

Sounds – The song is a mixture of whistles, trills, and chatters. The call is a "kip."

Diet – Insects, spiders, and berries are eaten.

Season found in Texas – East Texas can see this bird in the fall and winter.

Woodhouse's Scrub-Jay
Aphelocoma woodhouseii

Rapid Identification – The head, wings, and tail are a beautiful light blue, while the back is gray and the belly is white. The area around the eyes is dark, the bill is black, and the throat is white with a thin blue border below it. The long tail is blue with dark edges. Juveniles have less blue on the head.

Sounds – The song is a mix of notes lasting up to 5 minutes. The call is a rough shriek.

Diet – Insects, fruits, nuts, reptiles, and young birds are eaten.

Season found in Texas – Parts of central, north, and west Texas may see this bird year-round.

Yellow-bellied Sapsucker
(*Sphyrapicus varius*)

Male　　　Female　　　Male　　　Female

Rapid Identification – Males have a red patch on top of the head, bordered by black below. The eyes have a white stripe above them and a black stripe through them. A white stripe is beneath the eyes, and the throat is red with a black border. Some yellow may be seen below the throat. Females have a white throat instead of the red seen in males. The belly is mostly white to pale yellow with some black spots, and the back is black with white spots. The wings are black with a large white wing patch. The tail is short, black, and used as a prop against trees. Juveniles lack the red and look dirty.

Sounds – The call is described as a mewing call. The drumming of this bird is irregular and sounds like someone is tapping out morse code.

Diet – This woodpecker makes holes in trees so they can eat the sap that seeps from them.

Season found in Texas – Most of Texas, but not the northern and far western parts of Texas, will see this woodpecker.

Yellow-billed Cuckoo
Coccyzus americanus

Rapid Identification – This is a long, slender bird that is brown above and white below. The top half of the beak is black, and the bottom half is yellow. The tail is long and thin, with large white spots on a black background. Rust colored patches may be seen in the wings.

Sounds – The Yellow-billed cuckoo has a loud call that often gives away its position. It is described as a guttural "ka, ka, ka, ka, ka, kow, kow, kow, kowlp, kowlp), lasting about eight seconds.

Diet – Caterpillars are the favorite prey item for this bird. They will also consume spiders, ants, beetles, crickets, frogs, lizards, fruits, and berries.

Season found in Texas – Spring and summer throughout the state.

Yellow-breasted Chat (*Icteria virens*)

Rapid Identification – The head and throat of this bird look a bit large when compared to most birds. Most of this bird's head is gray, but there is a white patch above and below the eyes, with a dark patch between the two in front of the eyes. A thin white eye ring is visible if you can get close enough to see it. The throat, chest, and much of the belly are yellow, and the lower part of the belly is white. The top of the head, back, wings, and long tail are gray to olive-gray. The wings have yellow mixed in with the dark colors, and in flight, the yellow is easy to see.

Sounds – Songs are made up of whistles, squawks, and many irregular sounds. Calls may be a scolding "mew" or a double "chew-chew."

Diet – Insects, spiders, fruits, and berries are all eaten.

Season found in Texas – Parts of western, central, and eastern Texas may see this bird in the spring and summer. Other regions will only see them as they migrate through.

Yellow-headed Blackbird
(*Xanthocephalus xanthocephalus*)

Rapid Identification – For males, the head, neck, and chest are golden yellow. The beak is black, and a black mask is found between the eyes and beak. The rest of the bird is black, except for a white patch on each wing. The female is brown instead of black and has far less yellow than the male.

Sounds – Males sing a short song that sounds like the movement of rusty metal hinges. Females make short chattering sounds. A rapid and short "check" call is made during the breading season.

Diet – Insects are consumed more in the spring and summer, while seeds are taken the rest of the year. Beetles, grasshoppers, crickets, spiders, dragonflies, and more are commonly eaten.

Season found in Texas – Migratory through most of the state. Fall and winter on the western edge.

215

Yellow-rumped Warbler (*Setophaga coronate*)

Male Female

Rapid Identification – A small bird with a mixture of yellow, gray, black (black mask), and white on the head. A yellow spot on the rump (on top, just before the tail) and yellow shoulder patches are good identifying marks. The back is a blue gray (slate), the chest is largely black, and the belly is white with dark stripes. Females have duller colors and are more brown than blue gray.
This is the Myrtle form of the bird.

Sounds – The song is a series of rapid whistles that fall off at the end. The calls are a sharp "chek" or "tink".

Female Male

Diet – Insects and berries.

Season found in Texas – Fall and winter throughout the state.

216

Yellow-throated Vireo (*Vireo flavifrons*)

Rapid Identification – The head, back, and flanks are dark yellow to olive-green. The area around the eyes and between the eyes and the bill is not dark but bright yellow. A dark line runs from the eyes to the bill. The throat, chest, and top half of the belly are yellow, and the lower half of the belly is white. The chest and belly may have some dark patches. The wings are dark, with two white wingbars and white vertical streaks.

Sounds – The song is a mixture of two and three-syllable whistles. The call is a chatter that sounds like laughter.

Diet – Insects, spiders, seeds, and fruits are eaten.

Season found in Texas – South and east Texas can see this bird in the spring and summer.

Yellow-throated Warbler
(*Setophaga dominica*)

Rapid Identification – The top of the head is black with a white line beneath it. The eyes have a dark line behind them, a dark patch around them (face mask), a dark patch beneath them, and a white crescent beneath them. The throat and top of the chest are bright yellow. The lower half of the chest and belly are white, while the flanks are white with black streaks. The back is blue-gray, and the wings have the same color with two white wingbars. From above, the tail is the same color as the back. From below, the tail is white with dark tips.

Sounds – The call is a series of 10 or so high-pitched notes. The call is a soft chip.

Diet – Insects are eaten by this bird.

Season found in Texas – East Texas can see this bird in spring and summer.

Yellow Warbler (*Setophaga petechia*)

Rapid Identification – Males are a bright yellow over most of the body. The small eyes are black, the bill is black, and the back is yellow-green. The chest and belly have rusty vertical streaks. The wings are yellow with dark streaks. The tail is yellow, with the lateral feathers being dark. The yellow on females is not as bright, and the streaks on the chest are absent. Immature birds are more of a grayish yellow.

Sounds – The song is a musical "sweet-sweet-sweet-I'm so sweet." Calls are quick "chips."

Diet – Insects such as beetles and wasps are eaten by this bird.

Season found in Texas – All of Texas may see this bird as it migrates through.

Zone-tailed Hawk (*Buteo albonotatus*)

Rapid Identification – This is a dark raptor with yellow legs and a bill that is yellow close to the face and black at the sharply angled tip. From below, the leading edge of the wings is black, most of the feathers are white with black bars, and the trailing edge has a black border. From below, the tail is also black with a broad white band. They are often mistaken for turkey vultures, but the white band on the tail will allow you to tell them apart.

Sounds – The call is a long "kreeeeee."

Diet – This hawk will eat mammals, birds, reptiles, amphibians, and fish.

Season found in Texas – South and west Texas may see this hawk in the spring and summer.

References

10 Fun Facts About the Pileated Woodpecker. (2022, July 19). Audubon. https://www.audubon.org/news/10-fun-facts-about-pileated-woodpecker

American Crow Life History, All About Birds, Cornell Lab of Ornithology. (n.d.). https://www.allaboutbirds.org/guide/American_Crow/lifehistory

American Goldfinch Identification, All About Birds, Cornell Lab of Ornithology. (n.d.). https://www.allaboutbirds.org/guide/American_Goldfinch/id

American Pipit Overview, All about birds, Cornell Lab of Ornithology. (n.d.). https://www.allaboutbirds.org/guide/American_Pipit/overview

American RedStart Identification, All about Birds, Cornell Lab of Ornithology. (n.d.). https://www.allaboutbirds.org/guide/American_Redstart/id

American Robin Identification, All About Birds, Cornell Lab of Ornithology. (n.d.). https://www.allaboutbirds.org/guide/American_Robin/id

American Tree Sparrow Overview, All about birds, Cornell Lab of Ornithology. (n.d.). https://www.allaboutbirds.org/guide/american_tree_sparrow

Ash-throated flycatcher sounds, all about birds, Cornell Lab of Ornithology. (n.d.). https://www.allaboutbirds.org/guide/Ash-throated_Flycatcher/sounds

B. (2022a, May 18). *Female Starlings (Identification Guide)*. Birdfact. https://birdfact.com/birds/starling/female-starlings

Bank Swallow Life History, All about Birds, Cornell Lab of Ornithology. (n.d.). https://www.allaboutbirds.org/guide/Bank_Swallow/lifehistory

Barn Owl Identification, All About Birds, Cornell Lab of Ornithology. (n.d.). https://www.allaboutbirds.org/guide/Barn_Owl/id

Barn Owl Nest Box. (2020, December 2). *Male and Female Differences - Barn Owl Nest Box.* https://owlbox.live/barn-owl-information/sexing-males-and-females/male-and-female-differences/

Barn Swallow Overview, All About Birds, Cornell Lab of Ornithology. (n.d.). https://www.allaboutbirds.org/guide/barn_swallow

Barred Owl Life History, All About Birds, Cornell Lab of Ornithology. (n.d.). https://www.allaboutbirds.org/guide/Barred_Owl/lifehistory

Bell's Vireo Overview, All about birds, Cornell Lab of Ornithology. (n.d.). https://www.allaboutbirds.org/guide/Bells_Vireo/overview

Bewick's Wren Overview, All about Birds, Cornell Lab of Ornithology. (n.d.). https://www.allaboutbirds.org/guide/Bewicks_Wren/overview

Black-and-white Warbler Identification, All About Birds, Cornell Lab of Ornithology. (n.d.). https://www.allaboutbirds.org/guide/Black-and-white_Warbler/id

Black-capped Vireo Identification, All about Birds, Cornell Lab of Ornithology. (n.d.). https://www.allaboutbirds.org/guide/Black-capped_Vireo/id

Black-chinned Hummingbird overview, All about Birds, Cornell Lab of Ornithology. (n.d.). https://www.allaboutbirds.org/guide/Black-chinned_Hummingbird/overview

Black-crested Titmouse Overview, All about birds, Cornell Lab of Ornithology. (n.d.). https://www.allaboutbirds.org/guide/Black-crested_Titmouse

Black-headed Grosbeak Overview, All about birds, Cornell Lab of Ornithology. (n.d.). https://www.allaboutbirds.org/guide/Black-headed_Grosbeak/overview

Black-tailed Gnatcatcher Identification, All about Birds, Cornell Lab of Ornithology. (n.d.). https://www.allaboutbirds.org/guide/Black-tailed_Gnatcatcher/id

Black-throated sparrow identification, All about Birds, Cornell Lab of Ornithology. (n.d.). https://www.allaboutbirds.org/guide/Black-throated_Sparrow/id

Blue-gray Gnatcatcher Overview, All about birds, Cornell Lab of Ornithology. (n.d.). https://www.allaboutbirds.org/guide/Blue-gray_Gnatcatcher/overview

Blue Grosbeak Identification, All About Birds, Cornell Lab of Ornithology. (n.d.). Blue Grosbeak Identification, All About Birds, Cornell Lab of Ornithology. https://www.allaboutbirds.org/guide/Blue_Grosbeak/id

Blue-headed Vireo Overview, All about birds, Cornell Lab of Ornithology. (n.d.). https://www.allaboutbirds.org/guide/Blue-headed_Vireo

Blue Jay Identification, All About Birds, Cornell Lab of Ornithology. (n.d.). https://www.allaboutbirds.org/guide/Blue_Jay/id

Blue Jay. Audubon Field Guide. https://www.audubon.org/field-guide/bird/blue-jay

Brewer's Blackbird Overview, All about birds, Cornell Lab of Ornithology. (n.d.). https://www.allaboutbirds.org/guide/Brewers_Blackbird/overview

Brewer's Sparrow Overview, All about birds, Cornell Lab of Ornithology. (n.d.). https://www.allaboutbirds.org/guide/Brewers_Sparrow

Broad-winged Hawk Life History, All about birds, Cornell Lab of Ornithology. (n.d.). https://www.allaboutbirds.org/guide/Broad-winged_Hawk/lifehistory

Bronzed Cowbird Identification, All about Birds, Cornell Lab of Ornithology. (n.d.). https://www.allaboutbirds.org/guide/Bronzed_Cowbird/id

Brown Creeper Overview, All about Birds, Cornell Lab of Ornithology. (n.d.). https://www.allaboutbirds.org/guide/Brown_Creeper/overview

Brown-crested Flycatcher Overview, All about birds, Cornell Lab of Ornithology. (n.d.). https://www.allaboutbirds.org/guide/Brown-crested_Flycatcher/overview

Brown-headed Cowbird Identification, All About Birds, Cornell Lab of Ornithology. (n.d.). https://www.allaboutbirds.org/guide/Brown-headed_Cowbird/id

Brown-headed Nuthatch Identification, All About Birds, Cornell Lab of Ornithology. (n.d.). https://www.allaboutbirds.org/guide/Brown-headed_Nuthatch/id

Brown Thrasher. (n.d.). Audubon. https://www.audubon.org/field-guide/bird/brown-thrasher

Brown Thrasher Overview, All About Birds, Cornell Lab of Ornithology. (n.d.). https://www.allaboutbirds.org/guide/Brown_Thrasher/overview

Bullock's Oriole Overview, All about Birds, Cornell Lab of Ornithology. (n.d.). https://www.allaboutbirds.org/guide/Bullocks_Oriole/overview

Bushtit Overview, All about birds, Cornell Lab of Ornithology. (n.d.). https://www.allaboutbirds.org/guide/Bushtit/overview

Cactus Wren Overview, All about Birds, Cornell Lab of Ornithology. (n.d.). https://www.allaboutbirds.org/guide/Cactus_Wren/overview

Canyon Towhee Overview, All about birds, Cornell Lab of Ornithology. (n.d.). https://www.allaboutbirds.org/guide/Canyon_Towhee

Canyon Wren Overview, All about birds, Cornell Lab of Ornithology. (n.d.). https://www.allaboutbirds.org/guide/canyon_wren

Carolina Chickadee Identification, All About Birds, Cornell Lab of Ornithology. (n.d.). https://www.allaboutbirds.org/guide/Carolina_Chickadee/id

Carolina Wren. (2021, October 20). Audubon. https://www.audubon.org/field-guide/bird/carolina-wren

Carolina Wren Overview, All About Birds, Cornell Lab of Ornithology. (n.d.). https://www.allaboutbirds.org/guide/carolina_wren

Cedar Waxwing Sounds, All About Birds, Cornell Lab of Ornithology. (n.d.). https://www.allaboutbirds.org/guide/Cedar_Waxwing/sounds

Chestnut-collared Longspur Overview, All about birds, Cornell Lab of Ornithology. (n.d.). https://www.allaboutbirds.org/guide/Chestnut-collared_Longspur

Chihuahuan Raven Overview, All about Birds, Cornell Lab of Ornithology. (n.d.). https://www.allaboutbirds.org/guide/Chihuahuan_Raven/overview

Chimney Swift Identification, All About Birds, Cornell Lab of Ornithology. (n.d.). https://www.allaboutbirds.org/guide/Chimney_Swift/id

Chimney Swift. (n.d.). Audubon. https://www.audubon.org/field-guide/bird/chimney-swift

Chipping Sparrow Life History, All About Birds, Cornell Lab of Ornithology. (n.d.). https://www.allaboutbirds.org/guide/Chipping_Sparrow/lifehistory

Clay-colored Sparrow Overview, All about birds, Cornell Lab of Ornithology. (n.d.). https://www.allaboutbirds.org/guide/Clay-colored_Sparrow/overview

Cliff Swallow Overview, All about birds, Cornell Lab of Ornithology. (n.d.). https://www.allaboutbirds.org/guide/Cliff_Swallow/overview

Common Grackle Overview, All About Birds, Cornell Lab of Ornithology. (n.d.). https://www.allaboutbirds.org/guide/Common_Grackle/overview

Common Ground Dove Overview, All about birds, Cornell Lab of Ornithology. (n.d.). https://www.allaboutbirds.org/guide/common_ground_dove

Common Raven identification, All about Birds, Cornell Lab of Ornithology. (n.d.). https://www.allaboutbirds.org/guide/Common_Raven/id

Common Yellowthroat Identification, All About Birds, Cornell Lab of Ornithology. (n.d.). https://www.allaboutbirds.org/guide/Common_Yellowthroat/id

Couch's Kingbird Overview, All about birds, Cornell Lab of Ornithology. (n.d.). https://www.allaboutbirds.org/guide/Couchs_Kingbird/overview

Curve-billed Thrasher Overview, All about Birds, Cornell Lab of Ornithology. (n.d.). https://www.allaboutbirds.org/guide/Curve-billed_Thrasher/overview

Dickcissel Life History, All about Birds, Cornell Lab of Ornithology. (n.d.). https://www.allaboutbirds.org/guide/Dickcissel/lifehistory

Downy Woodpecker Identification, All About Birds, Cornell Lab of Ornithology. (n.d.). https://www.allaboutbirds.org/guide/Downy_Woodpecker/id

Cooper's Hawk Identification, All About Birds, Cornell Lab of Ornithology. (n.d.). https://www.allaboutbirds.org/guide/Coopers_Hawk/id

Eastern Bluebird Overview, All About Birds, Cornell Lab of Ornithology. (n.d.). https://www.allaboutbirds.org/guide/Eastern_Bluebird/overview

Editor. (2022, December 8). Common grackle. Bird Informer. https://www.birdinformer.com/field-guide/common-grackle/

Eastern Kingbird Overview, All About Birds, Cornell Lab of Ornithology. (n.d.). https://www.allaboutbirds.org/guide/Eastern_Kingbird/overview

Eastern Meadowlark. (n.d.). Audubon. https://www.audubon.org/field-guide/bird/eastern-meadowlark

Eastern Meadowlark Sounds, All About Birds, Cornell Lab of Ornithology. (n.d.). https://www.allaboutbirds.org/guide/Eastern_Meadowlark/sounds

Eastern Phoebe Identification, All About Birds, Cornell Lab of Ornithology. (n.d.). https://www.allaboutbirds.org/guide/Eastern_Phoebe/id

Eastern Screech-Owl. (n.d.). Audubon. https://www.audubon.org/field-guide/bird/eastern-screech-owl

Eastern Screech-Owl Identification, All About Birds, Cornell Lab of Ornithology. (n.d.). https://www.allaboutbirds.org/guide/Eastern_Screech-Owl/id

Eastern Towhee Identification, All About Birds, Cornell Lab of Ornithology. (n.d.). https://www.allaboutbirds.org/guide/Eastern_Towhee/id

Eastern Wood-Pewee Overview, All about birds, Cornell Lab of Ornithology. (n.d.). https://www.allaboutbirds.org/guide/Eastern_Wood-Pewee#

Editor. (2022, December 8). *White-throated sparrow - Bird Informer*. Bird Informer. https://www.birdinformer.com/field-guide/white-throated-sparrow/

Elf Owl Overview, All about Birds, Cornell Lab of Ornithology. (n.d.). https://www.allaboutbirds.org/guide/Elf_Owl

Eurasian Collared-Dove Identification, All About Birds, Cornell Lab of Ornithology. (n.d.). Eurasian Collared-Dove Identification, All About Birds, Cornell Lab of Ornithology. https://www.allaboutbirds.org/guide/Eurasian_Collared-Dove/id

European Starling Identification, All About Birds, Cornell Lab of Ornithology. (n.d.). https://www.allaboutbirds.org/guide/European_Starling/id

Evening Grosbeak Life History, All About Birds, Cornell Lab of Ornithology. (n.d.). https://www.allaboutbirds.org/guide/Evening_Grosbeak/lifehistory

Ferruginous Hawk Overview, All about birds, Cornell Lab of Ornithology. (n.d.). https://www.allaboutbirds.org/guide/Ferruginous_Hawk

Gray Catbird Identification, All About Birds, Cornell Lab of Ornithology. (n.d.). https://www.allaboutbirds.org/guide/Gray_Catbird/id

Field Sparrow Overview, All about birds, Cornell Lab of Ornithology. (n.d.). https://www.allaboutbirds.org/guide/field_sparrow

Fox Sparrow Overview, All About Birds, Cornell Lab of Ornithology. (n.d.). https://www.allaboutbirds.org/guide/Fox_Sparrow/overview

Golden-cheeked Warbler Life History, All about Birds, Cornell Lab of Ornithology. (n.d.). https://www.allaboutbirds.org/guide/Golden-cheeked_Warbler/lifehistory

Golden-fronted Woodpecker Life History, All about birds, Cornell Lab of Ornithology. (n.d.). https://www.allaboutbirds.org/guide/Golden-fronted_Woodpecker/lifehistory

Grasshopper Sparrow Overview, All about birds, Cornell Lab of Ornithology. (n.d.). https://www.allaboutbirds.org/guide/Grasshopper_Sparrow

Gray Hawk Overview, All about Birds, Cornell Lab of Ornithology. (n.d.). https://www.allaboutbirds.org/guide/gray_hawk

Great Crested Flycatcher Life History, All about birds, Cornell Lab of Ornithology. (n.d.). https://www.allaboutbirds.org/guide/Great_Crested_Flycatcher/lifehistory

Greater Roadrunner Overview, All about birds, Cornell Lab of Ornithology. (n.d.). https://www.allaboutbirds.org/guide/greater_roadrunner

Great Horned Owl. (n.d.). Audubon. https://www.audubon.org/field-guide/bird/great-horned-owl

Great Horned Owl Identification, All About Birds, Cornell Lab of Ornithology. (n.d.). https://www.allaboutbirds.org/guide/Great_Horned_Owl/id

Great-tailed Grackle Overview, All about birds, Cornell Lab of Ornithology. (n.d.). https://www.allaboutbirds.org/guide/Great-tailed_Grackle

Green Jay Overview, All about Birds, Cornell Lab of Ornithology. (n.d.). https://www.allaboutbirds.org/guide/green_jay

Green Kingfisher Overview, All about birds, Cornell Lab of Ornithology. (n.d.). https://www.allaboutbirds.org/guide/Green_Kingfisher

Green-tailed Towhee Overview, All about birds, Cornell Lab of Ornithology. (n.d.). https://www.allaboutbirds.org/guide/Green-tailed_Towhee

Harris's Hawk Overview, All about Birds, Cornell Lab of Ornithology. (n.d.). https://www.allaboutbirds.org/guide/Harriss_Hawk/overview

Harris's Sparrow Overview, All about birds, Cornell Lab of Ornithology. (n.d.). https://www.allaboutbirds.org/guide/Harriss_Sparrow/overview

Hepatic tanager Overview, All about Birds, Cornell Lab of Ornithology. (n.d.). https://www.allaboutbirds.org/guide/hepatic_tanager

Hermit Thrush Life History, All about Birds, Cornell Lab of Ornithology. (n.d.). https://www.allaboutbirds.org/guide/Hermit_Thrush/lifehistory

Hooded Oriole Overview, All about birds, Cornell Lab of Ornithology. (n.d.). https://www.allaboutbirds.org/guide/Hooded_Oriole

Horned Lark Overview, All about Birds, Cornell Lab of Ornithology. (n.d.). https://www.allaboutbirds.org/guide/horned_lark

House Finch Identification, All About Birds, Cornell Lab of Ornithology. (n.d.). https://www.allaboutbirds.org/guide/House_Finch/id

House Wren Identification, All About Birds, Cornell Lab of Ornithology. (n.d.). https://www.allaboutbirds.org/guide/House_Wren/id

House Sparrow Overview, All About Birds, Cornell Lab of Ornithology. (n.d.). https://www.allaboutbirds.org/guide/House_Sparrow/overview

Indigo Bunting Sounds, All About Birds, Cornell Lab of Ornithology. (n.d.). https://www.allaboutbirds.org/guide/Indigo_Bunting/sounds

Kaufman, K. (2016, April 21). *How to Identify Birds*. Audobon. https://www.audubon.org/news/how-identify-birds

Kaufman, K. (n.d.-a). *Barn Owl*. Audubon Guide to North American Birds. https://www.audubon.org/field-guide/bird/barn-owl

Kaufman, K. (n.d.). *Dark-eyed Junco*. Audubon Field Guide. https://www.audubon.org/field-guide/bird/dark-eyed-junco

Kaufman, K. (n.d.-b). *Downy woodpecker*. Audubon Guide to North American Birds. https://www.audubon.org/field-guide/bird/downy-woodpecker

Kaufman, K. (n.d.-c). *Gray Catbird*. Audubon Field Guide. https://www.audubon.org/field-guide/bird/gray-catbird

Kaufman, K. (n.d.). *House Wren*. Audubon Guide to North American Birds. https://www.audubon.org/field-guide/bird/house-wren

Ladder-backed Woodpecker Overview, All about birds, Cornell Lab of Ornithology. (n.d.). https://www.allaboutbirds.org/guide/Ladder-backed_Woodpecker/overview

Lark Bunting Overview, All about Birds, Cornell Lab of Ornithology. (n.d.). https://www.allaboutbirds.org/guide/lark_bunting

Lark Sparrow Overview, All about Birds, Cornell Lab of Ornithology. (n.d.). https://www.allaboutbirds.org/guide/Lark_Sparrow

Lazuli Bunting Overview, All about Birds, Cornell Lab of Ornithology. (n.d.). https://www.allaboutbirds.org/guide/Lazuli_Bunting/overview

Least Flycatcher Life History, All about birds, Cornell Lab of Ornithology. (n.d.). https://www.allaboutbirds.org/guide/Least_Flycatcher/lifehistory

LeConte's Sparrow Life History, All about birds, Cornell Lab of Ornithology. (n.d.). https://www.allaboutbirds.org/guide/LeContes_Sparrow/lifehistory

Lesser Goldfinch Life History, All about Birds, Cornell Lab of Ornithology. (n.d.). https://www.allaboutbirds.org/guide/Lesser_Goldfinch/lifehistory

Lincoln's Sparrow Overview, All about Birds, Cornell Lab of Ornithology. (n.d.). https://www.allaboutbirds.org/guide/Lincolns_Sparrow#

Loggerhead Shrike Overview, All About Birds, Cornell Lab of Ornithology. (n.d.). Loggerhead Shrike Overview, All About Birds, Cornell Lab of Ornithology. https://www.allaboutbirds.org/guide/Loggerhead_Shrike/overview

Long-billed Thrasher Overview, All about birds, Cornell Lab of Ornithology. (n.d.). https://www.allaboutbirds.org/guide/Long-billed_Thrasher/overview

Louisiana Waterthrush Sounds, All About Birds, Cornell Lab of Ornithology. (n.d.). Louisiana Waterthrush Sounds, All About Birds, Cornell Lab of Ornithology. https://www.allaboutbirds.org/guide/Louisiana_Waterthrush/sounds

Lund, N. (2023, February 21). *Birdist Rule #59: Learn to Identify Warblers From Below*. Audubon. https://www.audubon.org/news/birdist-rule-59-learn-identify-warblers-below

M. (2022, October 14). *Extraordinary Appendages: An Introduction to Bird Wings*. American Bird Conservancy. https://abcbirds.org/blog/bird-wings/

MacGillivray's Warbler Overview, All about Birds, Cornell Lab of Ornithology. (n.d.). https://www.allaboutbirds.org/guide/MacGillivrays_Warbler

Marsh Wren Overview, All about Birds, Cornell Lab of Ornithology. (n.d.). https://www.allaboutbirds.org/guide/Marsh_Wren

Mountain Bluebird Overview, All about birds, Cornell Lab of Ornithology. (n.d.). https://www.allaboutbirds.org/guide/mountain_bluebird

Mourning Dove Identification, All About Birds, Cornell Lab of Ornithology. (n.d.). https://www.allaboutbirds.org/guide/Mourning_Dove/id

Mechem, K. (2023, February 21). *How to Tell a Hairy Woodpecker From a Downy Woodpecker*. Audubon. https://www.audubon.org/news/how-tell-hairy-woodpecker-downy-woodpecker

Nashville Warbler Overview, All about birds, Cornell Lab of Ornithology. (n.d.). https://www.allaboutbirds.org/guide/Nashville_Warbler/overview

Northern Cardinal. (2021, October 20). Audubon. https://www.audubon.org/field-guide/bird/northern-cardinal

Northern Cardinal Identification, All About Birds, Cornell Lab of Ornithology. (n.d.). https://www.allaboutbirds.org/guide/Northern_Cardinal/id

Northern Flicker Identification, All About Birds, Cornell Lab of Ornithology. (n.d.). https://www.allaboutbirds.org/guide/Northern_Flicker/id

Northern Mockingbird Identification, All About Birds, Cornell Lab of Ornithology. (n.d.). https://www.allaboutbirds.org/guide/Northern_Mockingbird/id

Northern Parula Overview, All about birds, Cornell Lab of Ornithology. (n.d.). https://www.allaboutbirds.org/guide/Northern_Parula/overview

Northern Rough-winged Swallow Overview, All about birds, Cornell Lab of Ornithology. (n.d.). https://www.allaboutbirds.org/guide/Northern_Rough-winged_Swallow

Northern Waterthrush Sounds, all about birds, Cornell Lab of Ornithology. (n.d.). https://www.allaboutbirds.org/guide/Northern_Waterthrush/sounds

Oldham, C. (2019, June 24). *Barn Swallow - Description, Habitat, Image, Diet, and Interesting Facts*. Animals Network. https://animals.net/barn-swallow/

Olive-sided Flycatcher Overview, All about birds, Cornell Lab of Ornithology. (n.d.). https://www.allaboutbirds.org/guide/Olive-sided_Flycatcher/overview

Olive Sparrow Overview, All About Birds, Cornell Lab of Ornithology. (n.d.). https://www.allaboutbirds.org/guide/Olive_Sparrow

Orchard Oriole Overview, All About Birds, Cornell Lab of Ornithology. (n.d.). https://www.allaboutbirds.org/guide/Orchard_Oriole/overview

Orange-crowned Warbler Overview, All About Birds, Cornell Lab of Ornithology. (n.d.). https://www.allaboutbirds.org/guide/Orange-crowned_Warbler

Ovenbird Overview, All About Birds, Cornell Lab of Ornithology. (n.d.). https://www.allaboutbirds.org/guide/Ovenbird/overview

Painted Bunting Sounds, All About Birds, Cornell Lab of Ornithology. (n.d.). Painted Bunting Sounds, All About Birds, Cornell Lab of Ornithology. https://www.allaboutbirds.org/guide/Painted_Bunting/sounds

Pileated Woodpecker Overview, All About Birds, Cornell Lab of Ornithology. (n.d.). https://www.allaboutbirds.org/guide/Pileated_Woodpecker/overview

Pine Siskin Life History, All About Birds, Cornell Lab of Ornithology. (n.d.). https://www.allaboutbirds.org/guide/Pine_Siskin/lifehistory

Pine Warbler. (n.d.). Audubon. https://www.audubon.org/field-guide/bird/pine-warbler

Prairie Falcon Overview, All About Birds, Cornell Lab of Ornithology. (n.d.). https://www.allaboutbirds.org/guide/Prairie_Falcon

Prothonotary Warbler Identification, All About Birds, Cornell Lab of Ornithology. (n.d.). Prothonotary Warbler Identification, All About Birds, Cornell Lab of Ornithology. https://www.allaboutbirds.org/guide/Prothonotary_Warbler/id

Purple Martin. (n.d.). Audubon. https://www.audubon.org/field-guide/bird/purple-martin

Purple Martin Identification, All About Birds, Cornell Lab of Ornithology. (n.d.). https://www.allaboutbirds.org/guide/Purple_Martin/id

Pyrrhuloxia Overview, All About Birds, Cornell Lab of Ornithology. (n.d.). https://www.allaboutbirds.org/guide/Pyrrhuloxia

Red-bellied Woodpecker. (n.d.). Audubon. https://www.audubon.org/field-guide/bird/red-bellied-woodpecker

Red-bellied Woodpecker Identification, All About Birds, Cornell Lab of Ornithology. (n.d.). https://www.allaboutbirds.org/guide/Red-bellied_Woodpecker/id

Red-breasted Nuthatch Identification, All About Birds, Cornell Lab of Ornithology. (n.d.). https://www.allaboutbirds.org/guide/Red-breasted_Nuthatch/id

Red Crossbill Identification, All About Birds, Cornell Lab of Ornithology. (n.d.). https://www.allaboutbirds.org/guide/Red_Crossbill/id

Red-eyed Vireo Overview, All About Birds, Cornell Lab of Ornithology. (n.d.). https://www.allaboutbirds.org/guide/Red-eyed_Vireo

Red-headed Woodpecker Identification, All About Birds, Cornell Lab of Ornithology. (n.d.). https://www.allaboutbirds.org/guide/Red-headed_Woodpecker/id

Red-headed Woodpecker. (n.d.). Audubon. https://www.audubon.org/field-guide/bird/red-headed-woodpecker

Red-shouldered Hawk. (n.d.). Audubon. https://www.audubon.org/field-guide/bird/red-shouldered-hawk

Red-shouldered Hawk Identification, All About Birds, Cornell Lab of Ornithology. (n.d.). https://www.allaboutbirds.org/guide/Red-shouldered_Hawk/id

Red-tailed Hawk Life History, All About Birds, Cornell Lab of Ornithology. (n.d.). https://www.allaboutbirds.org/guide/Red-tailed_Hawk/lifehistory

Red-tailed Hawk. (n.d.). Audubon. https://www.audubon.org/field-guide/bird/red-tailed-hawk

Red-winged Blackbird. (2022, December 16). Audubon. https://www.audubon.org/field-guide/bird/red-winged-blackbird

Red-winged Blackbird Identification, All About Birds, Cornell Lab of Ornithology. (n.d.). https://www.allaboutbirds.org/guide/Red-winged_Blackbird/id

Rock Wren Overview, All About Birds, Cornell Lab of Ornithology. (n.d.). https://www.allaboutbirds.org/guide/rock_wren

Ruby-crowned Kinglet Identification, All About Birds, Cornell Lab of Ornithology. (n.d.). https://www.allaboutbirds.org/guide/Ruby-crowned_Kinglet/id

Ruby-throated Hummingbird Overview, All About Birds, Cornell Lab of Ornithology. (n.d.). https://www.allaboutbirds.org/guide/Ruby-throated_Hummingbird/overview

Rufous-crowned Sparrow Overview, All About Birds, Cornell Lab of Ornithology. (n.d.). https://www.allaboutbirds.org/guide/Rufous-crowned_Sparrow

Rufous Hummingbird Sounds, All About Birds, Cornell Lab of Ornithology. (n.d.). https://www.allaboutbirds.org/guide/Rufous_Hummingbird/sounds

Rusty Blackbird Life History, All About Birds, Cornell Lab of Ornithology. (n.d.). https://www.allaboutbirds.org/guide/Rusty_Blackbird/lifehistory

S. (2022, September 26). What Do Northern Flicker Calls Sound Like: Song & Sounds. SongbirdHub. https://songbirdhub.com/northern-flicker-call/

Sage Thrasher Overview, All About Birds, Cornell Lab of Ornithology. (n.d.). https://www.allaboutbirds.org/guide/Sage_Thrasher

Savannah Sparrow Life History, All About Birds, Cornell Lab of Ornithology. (n.d.). https://www.allaboutbirds.org/guide/Savannah_Sparrow/lifehistory

Say's Phoebe Overview, All About Birds, Cornell Lab of Ornithology. (n.d.). https://www.allaboutbirds.org/guide/Says_Phoebe

Scissor-tailed Flycatcher Identification, All About Birds, Cornell Lab of Ornithology. (n.d.). https://www.allaboutbirds.org/guide/Scissor-tailed_Flycatcher/id

Scissor-tailed Flycatcher. (n.d.). Audubon. https://www.audubon.org/field-guide/bird/scissor-tailed-flycatcher

Scott's Oriole Life History, All about Birds, Cornell Lab of Ornithology. (n.d.). https://www.allaboutbirds.org/guide/Scotts_Oriole/lifehistory

Song Sparrow Identification, All About Birds, Cornell Lab of Ornithology. (n.d.). https://www.allaboutbirds.org/guide/Song_Sparrow/id

Spotted Towhee Overview, All About Birds, Cornell Lab of Ornithology. (n.d.). https://www.allaboutbirds.org/guide/Spotted_Towhee#

Swamp Sparrow Life History, All About Birds, Cornell Lab of Ornithology. (n.d.). https://www.allaboutbirds.org/guide/Swamp_Sparrow/lifehistory

Summer Tanager Sounds, All About Birds, Cornell Lab of Ornithology. (n.d.). https://www.allaboutbirds.org/guide/Summer_Tanager/sounds

Tufted Titmouse Sounds, All About Birds, Cornell Lab of Ornithology. (n.d.). https://www.allaboutbirds.org/guide/Tufted_Titmouse/sounds

Townsend's Warbler Overview, All About Birds, Cornell Lab of Ornithology. (n.d.). https://www.allaboutbirds.org/guide/Townsends_Warbler

Tree Swallow Identification, All About Birds, Cornell Lab of Ornithology. (n.d.). https://www.allaboutbirds.org/guide/Tree_Swallow/id

Varied bunting overview, All about Birds, Cornell Lab of Ornithology. (n.d.). https://www.allaboutbirds.org/guide/varied_bunting#

Verdin Life History, All about Birds, Cornell Lab of Ornithology. (n.d.). https://www.allaboutbirds.org/guide/Verdin/lifehistory

Vermilion Flycatcher Overview, All about birds, Cornell Lab of Ornithology. (n.d.). https://www.allaboutbirds.org/guide/Vermilion_Flycatcher

Vesper Sparrow Sounds, All about Birds, Cornell Lab of Ornithology. (n.d.). https://www.allaboutbirds.org/guide/Vesper_Sparrow/sounds

Violet-green Swallow Life History, All About Birds, Cornell Lab of Ornithology. (n.d.). https://www.allaboutbirds.org/guide/Violet-green_Swallow/lifehistory

Warbling Vireo Sounds, All About Birds, Cornell Lab of Ornithology. (n.d.). https://www.allaboutbirds.org/guide/Warbling_Vireo/sounds

Western Kingbird Life History, All About Birds, Cornell Lab of Ornithology. (n.d.). https://www.allaboutbirds.org/guide/Western_Kingbird/lifehistory

Western Meadowlark Life History, All About Birds, Cornell Lab of Ornithology. (n.d.). https://www.allaboutbirds.org/guide/Western_Meadowlark/lifehistory

Western Screech-Owl Overview, All About Birds, Cornell Lab of Ornithology. (n.d.). https://www.allaboutbirds.org/guide/Western_Screech-Owl

Western Tanager Life History, All About Birds, Cornell Lab of Ornithology. (n.d.). https://www.allaboutbirds.org/guide/Western_Tanager/lifehistory

Western Wood-Pewee Sounds, All About Birds, Cornell Lab of Ornithology. (n.d.). https://www.allaboutbirds.org/guide/Western_Wood-Pewee/sounds

White-breasted Nuthatch Identification, All About Birds, Cornell Lab of Ornithology. (n.d.). https://www.allaboutbirds.org/guide/White-breasted_Nuthatch/id

White-breasted Nuthatch. (n.d.). Audubon. https://www.audubon.org/field-guide/bird/white-breasted-nuthatch

White-crowned Sparrow. (n.d.). Audubon. https://www.audubon.org/field-guide/bird/white-crowned-sparrow

White-crowned Sparrow Range Map, All About Birds, Cornell Lab of Ornithology. (n.d.). https://www.allaboutbirds.org/guide/White-crowned_Sparrow/maps-range

White-eyed Vireo Identification, All About Birds, Cornell Lab of Ornithology. (n.d.). https://www.allaboutbirds.org/guide/White-eyed_Vireo/id

White-tailed Kite Identification, All About Birds, Cornell Lab of Ornithology. (n.d.). https://www.allaboutbirds.org/guide/White-tailed_Kite/id

White-throated Sparrow Overview, All About Birds, Cornell Lab of Ornithology. (n.d.). https://www.allaboutbirds.org/guide/White-throated_Sparrow/

White-tipped Dove Identification, All About Birds, Cornell Lab of Ornithology. (n.d.). https://www.allaboutbirds.org/guide/White-tipped_Dove/id

White-winged Dove Overview, All About Birds, Cornell Lab of Ornithology. (n.d.). White-winged Dove Overview, All About Birds, Cornell Lab of Ornithology. https://www.allaboutbirds.org/guide/White-winged_Dove/overview

Willow Flycatcher Overview, All About Birds, Cornell Lab of Ornithology. (n.d.). https://www.allaboutbirds.org/guide/Willow_Flycatcher

Wilson's Warbler Overview, All About Birds, Cornell Lab of Ornithology. (n.d.). https://www.allaboutbirds.org/guide/Wilsons_Warbler/overview

Winter Wren Identification, All About Birds, Cornell Lab of Ornithology. (n.d.). https://www.allaboutbirds.org/guide/Winter_Wren/id

Woodhouse's Scrub-Jay Identification, All About Birds, Cornell Lab of Ornithology. (n.d.). https://www.allaboutbirds.org/guide/Woodhouses_Scrub-Jay/id

Yellow-bellied Sapsucker Sounds, All About Birds, Cornell Lab of Ornithology. (n.d.). https://www.allaboutbirds.org/guide/Yellow-bellied_Sapsucker/sounds

Yellow-billed Cuckoo Sounds, All About Birds, Cornell Lab of Ornithology. (n.d.). Yellow-billed Cuckoo Sounds, All About Birds, Cornell Lab of Ornithology. https://www.allaboutbirds.org/guide/Yellow-billed_Cuckoo/sounds

Yellow-breasted Chat Overview, All About Birds, Cornell Lab of Ornithology. (n.d.). https://www.allaboutbirds.org/guide/Yellow-breasted_Chat#

Yellow-headed Blackbird Overview, All About Birds, Cornell Lab of Ornithology. (n.d.). Yellow-headed Blackbird Overview, All About Birds, Cornell Lab of Ornithology. https://www.allaboutbirds.org/guide/Yellow-headed_Blackbird/overview

Yellow-rumped Warbler Sounds, All About Birds, Cornell Lab of Ornithology. (n.d.). https://www.allaboutbirds.org/guide/Yellow-rumped_Warbler/sounds

Yellow-throated Vireo Life History, All About Birds, Cornell Lab of Ornithology. (n.d.). https://www.allaboutbirds.org/guide/Yellow-throated_Vireo/lifehistory

Yellow-throated Warbler Overview, All About Birds, Cornell Lab of Ornithology. (n.d.). https://www.allaboutbirds.org/guide/Yellow-throated_Warbler

Yellow Warbler Overview, All About Birds, Cornell Lab of Ornithology. (n.d.). https://www.allaboutbirds.org/guide/Yellow_Warbler

Zone-tailed Hawk Overview, All About Birds, Cornell Lab of Ornithology. (n.d.). https://www.allaboutbirds.org/guide/Zone-tailed_Hawk

Made in the USA
Coppell, TX
07 April 2025